Religious Studies and the Goal of Interdisciplinarity

This book offers a survey of the development of interdisciplinarity in religious studies within academia and offers ways for it to continue to progress in contemporary universities. It examines the use of the term 'interdisciplinary' in the context of the academic study of religion and how it shapes the way scholarly work in this field has developed.

The text uses two main elements to discuss religious studies as a field. Firstly, it looks at the history of the development of religious studies in academia, as seen through an interdisciplinary critique of the university as an epistemological project. It then uses the same interdisciplinary critique to develop a foundation for a 21st-century hermeneutic, one which uses the classical concepts reprised by that interdisciplinary critique and retools the field for the 21st century.

Setting out both the objects of religious studies as a subject and the techniques used to employ the study of those objects, this book offers an invaluable perspective on the progress of the field. It will, therefore, be of great use to scholars of research methods within religious studies.

Brent Smith is an Associate Professor in the Liberal Studies Department at Grand Valley State University, USA.

Routledge Focus on Religion

Amoris Laetitia and the Spirit of Vatican II
The Source of Controversy
Mariusz Biliniewicz

Muslim and Jew
Origins, Growth, Resentment
Aaron W. Hughes

The Bible and Digital Millennials
David G. Ford, Joshua L. Mann and Peter M. Phillips

The Fourth Secularisation
Autonomy of Individual Lifestyles
Luigi Berzano

Narratives of Faith from the Haiti Earthquake
Religion, Natural Hazards and Disaster Response
Roger P. Abbott and Robert S. White

The Bible, Social Media and Digital Culture
Peter M. Phillips

Religious Studies and the Goal of Interdisciplinarity
Brent Smith

Visual Thought in Russian Religious Philosophy
Pavel Florensky's Theory of the Icon
Clemena Antonova

For more information about this series, please visit: www.routledge.com/
Routledge-Focus-on-Religion/book-series/RFR

Religious Studies and the Goal of Interdisciplinarity

Brent Smith

LONDON AND NEW YORK

First published 2020 by Routledge

2 Park Square, Milton Park, Abingdon, Oxon, OX14 4RN
605 Third Avenue, New York, NY 10017

Routledge is an imprint of the Taylor & Francis Group, an informa business

First issued in paperback 2020

Copyright © 2020 Brent Smith

The right of Brent Smith to be identified as author of this work has been asserted by him in accordance with sections 77 and 78 of the Copyright, Designs and Patents Act 1988.

All rights reserved. No part of this book may be reprinted or reproduced or utilised in any form or by any electronic, mechanical, or other means, now known or hereafter invented, including photocopying and recording, or in any information storage or retrieval system, without permission in writing from the publishers.

Notice:
Product or corporate names may be trademarks or registered trademarks, and are used only for identification and explanation without intent to infringe.

British Library Cataloguing-in-Publication Data
A catalogue record for this book is available from the British Library

Library of Congress Cataloging-in-Publication Data
A catalog record for this book has been requested

ISBN: 978-0-367-02944-9 (hbk)
ISBN: 978-0-367-78436-2 (pbk)

Typeset in Times New Roman
by Apex CoVantage, LLC

Contents

	Acknowledgements	vi
	Introduction: location, positionality, and the interdisciplinary religious studies scholar	1
1	Locating the academic study of religion: an interdisciplinary critique of the epistemological development of the university	23
2	Something other than an "and" or an "is": the overlapping domain of the sacred-profane	47
3	Sighting the sacred unseen: a camouflaged order appears	65
4	Hierophany as an interdisciplinary concept	83
5	A summary and summons	95
	Bibliography	101
	Index	107

Acknowledgements

Throughout my life I have been upheld, prodded, and inspired by so many, and this project is evidence that what I call "myself" involves an expanse of persons and places who shape(d) "me." My deepest gratitude goes to my wife, Pat, my emotional companion, constant intellectual mentor, and soulmate; my mother, Janet, who encouraged my curiosity and drive to know; and my two children, Elizabeth and Josh and those whom they and I love. Thank you David Tracy, my other intellectual mentor who understands interpretation, appreciates language, and teaches that the life of the mind involves following its interests. Thank you Peter S. Raible, John B. Wolf, and Suzanne Meyer, my professional mentors in the parish ministry, who each in their own way taught me to attend to the unseen, the moods and motivations and forces that energize people for good and ill. Thank you to other ministerial colleagues, especially Nicole Kirk, Earl Holt, Burton Carley, and the Prairie Group, who all kept my interest in scholarship strong while serving congregations. Thank you to the administrators at Grand Valley State University who graciously invited me into my academic location as I moved from one professional identity and life into another. A special thank you goes to Melanie Shell-Weiss, Wendy Burns-Ardolino, Sarah King, Abhishek Ghosh, Shel Kopperl, Diane Maodush-Pitzer, Anthony Meyer, Azfar Hussain, Marilyn Preston, Santos Ramos, and Judy Whipps who listened, gave feedback, and provided invaluable resources. Standing inside of the Religious Studies Program in the Department of Integrative, Religious, and Intercultural Studies of Brooks College of Interdisciplinary Studies means you navigate the waters of knowledge with those holding a different expertise and education but who, like you, share a vessel guided by an interdisciplinary sextant into the new space of uncharted waters. I am grateful for all those who have and still help guide me on my way.

Introduction

Location, positionality, and the interdisciplinary religious studies scholar

When asked to describe the academic study of religion to others, religious studies scholars frequently refer to it as being "interdisciplinary" without offering a comprehensive treatment of what that might mean. But, what does interdisciplinary mean? What are the characteristics of performing an interdisciplinary research inquiry, and how would those characteristics look in the academic study of religion? And, how does and should it shape the way the field goes about its tasks through the use of basic concepts? The themes and objectives of this book involve exploring that designation.

In this introduction readers will encounter the first descriptions of inter-disciplinarity, begin to identify the characteristics of the interdisciplinary scholar in religious studies (the most widespread name used in both the field and the university to designate of the current academic study of religion), and outline what each chapter will entail.

Interdisciplinarity integrates a two-step process in creating knowledge. First, interdisciplinarity involves a critique of how the university as an epistemological project has gathered and ordered knowledge throughout its historical development and has employed certain ways to disseminate the knowledge it produces. And secondly, within that critique interdisciplinar-ity generates a new space for knowledge production. Wherever in the university the interdisciplinary scholar is located, the scholar's positionality is not primarily from or out of a discipline or field, but interdisciplinarity is in relationship to the university as a whole and not a particular field or discipline. Thus, the interdisciplinary religious studies scholar performs the methodologies of religious studies through interdisciplinarity. As this book will suggest and discuss in more depth in the first chapter, interdisciplinarity is a style of performing the methodologies current in a field like religious studies. For example, there is a way to perform comparison, explanation, and hermeneutics that is interdisciplinary, and there is a way to perform those methodologies that is not.

2 Introduction

As a university location within which the modern embodiment of studying this activity in human existence, religious studies has developed out of previous endeavors and all were shaped by how the university historically and culturally has understood and performed its project. In this way the book locates religious studies within the context of a particular historical form and development in epistemology, the university approach to *how knowledge has been and is gathered and ordered and disseminated up to our own day*. This approach is part of the identity of religious studies in what it identifies as the concept of "religion," what the characteristics are of that at a given time in the history of the university and the cultures wherein it lies, how it studies what it characterizes as its object of study, and how contestations in these and all other areas are understood. Therefore, the interdisciplinary religious studies scholar pursues a self-consciousness about professional location and the way it overlaps with personal identities past and present. The location where religious studies emerged is as critical to scholars' professional self-identity as is my personal identity to my home state of Indiana, my hometown of Richmond, and the neighborhood of Southwest 16th Street even though I haven't lived there for nearly 50 years! Both the creation of the university and the origin of what is involved in the study of religion – from Christian theology to natural religion to the science of religions to religious studies – all of these shape what scholars do, think they should do, and think how they will go about doing what they think they should do. The epistemological development of the university not only gave religious studies its initial and central concepts, but shaped how they were understood and how they are and have been properly and improperly used.

The intellectual history of the university still does this. Most recently the history of the university and hence, the location within which religious studies finds itself as an academic field of study, has seen the privileging of science and social scientific concepts and methods in the gathering and ordering of knowledge, most specifically those from neurology, political science, and cultural studies. The second theme of this book acknowledges this most recent history and critiques it in how the university historically has housed the tension between three evaluative organizing principles which privilege certain kinds of knowledge: scientific, philosophical, and religion as variously understood relative to different eras in the history of the university. At different times in history each gained status over the other two even as they form contesting epistemological viewpoints. The university arose in 12th- and 13th-century Europe governed by the Christian theological ethos of its time, with philosophy and science as its servants. From the Renaissance through the Reformation philosophy gradually ascended to prominence until the Enlightenment saw its eminence over theology and science. During this time theology gained an "internal rival" in the creation

Introduction 3

of natural religion by philosophy, even as theology contended with philosophy for prominence. This creation of a new understanding of "religion" and of theology as a foe confirmed philosophy's privileged position. For the past two centuries the university has looked to science to unify its epistemological production, fulfilling the role of epistemic organizing principles that Christian theology and philosophy had previously. It is this epistemological construct that the academic study of religion arose as a perspective differentiated from its social scientific and philological roots, shaped by philosophy, contending with its internal rival theology, but as with other parts of the university, "measured" as of value by science. Social constructionist critique and an exhaustion of the pursuit of a "science of religion" left the focus of the academic study of religion on itself, how it was being practiced and who it was that was performing the practicing. One characteristic of the interdisciplinary style of performing methodology in religious studies is that the scholar identifies what is being done relative to a viewpoint of the history of the university and the field in relationship to that university history. This book is no different in that it describes the characteristics of interdisciplinarity by presenting a viewpoint on the history of the university (as an epistemological project) within which religious studies arose as a field of study.

In the past few decades new areas of study are pushing the academic study of religion beyond the social constructionist critique, beyond the concerns dictated by the modern university's scientific epistemic privileging, and towards how activities function religiously: what is called Material Religion, Religion and the Body, Lived Religion, approaches involving the Participatory Turn, etc. These contain an implicit intellectual foundation related to the university's epistemological context historically and yet push beyond the exclusivity of scientific, empirical privileging and the cultural reductionism that so much social constructionist critiques lean towards or yield. This book seeks to make explicit the epistemological foundation of these new areas of study as interdisciplinary to the extent they exhibit certain characteristics of that style. In doing this the book will reprise two classic concepts in religious studies – the sacred and profane, and the hierophany – by tracing their origin in the university of the late 19th through the 20th century, through the context of the university whose privileging of science increasingly evidenced a scienticism, to where each has come to be critiqued by social constructionism the last three decades. This tracing the historical development of concepts through the lens of a critique of the university as an epistemological project fulfills one characteristic of interdisciplinarity. Another characteristic, that it creates a new space for the creation of new knowledge, will be pursued in order to retool them intentionally and self-consciously for emerging new ventures in the field.

4 *Introduction*

In this way this book models the paradigm interdisciplinary performance to generate a creative reprisal of two basic concepts of religious studies to retool them for use in emerging studies in the field. And, to introduce a reconsideration of a third, the unseen order, as relevant to interdisciplinary work in religious studies in the 21st century. The characteristics of interdisciplinarity will be enumerated in the first chapter. These include the style in which (1) a more detailed presentation and critique of the intellectual development of the university shapes (2) the way in which an interdisciplinary scholar goes about the task of integrating disciplinary yields through self-conscious intentionality (in this author's case it will be disciplines of philosophy and the history of ideas, psychology, neurology, anthropology, geography, and sociology), interfaces with the engagement and framing of (3) an activity whose location is outside of and far away from the university location where concepts and methodologies are constructed, in order to (4) generate a new space for knowledge production concerning that activity as the scholar returns to the university to fulfill the interdisciplinary epistemological task: the integration of a variety of disciplines (history, the history of ideas, philosophy, sociology, anthropology) – as the intellectual foundation for new knowledge and understanding.

Thus, what you have before you is a book located in the field of the academic study of religion, religious studies in general, within a particular location, the university at this time in its development and as understood through interdisciplinary critique. The interdisciplinary scholar takes that location to locations outside of it in order to engage phenomena involving activities the scholar and the field inside the university have deemed "religious." This activity fulfills its temporary aim of producing a new space for knowledge when the scholar returns to the university setting in order to evaluate the way activity outside changes concepts designed inside, thereby creating new knowledge and contributing novel understanding.

The importance and complexity of location

As a professor in a religious studies program in a western Michigan public university, housed within an interdisciplinary college with its own unique creation history, I teach a course on the introduction to the academic study of religion for our majors/minors but which, in any given semester, will include students from other disciplines and areas of expertise. I teach it from a location shaped by my graduate education, my 27 years as a preacher and pulpit theologian in the Unitarian Universalist tradition, and now in a location firmly rooted in the field of the academic study of religion. I am the "concepts and methods" professor. In one class a student told me this story that sets an analogical foundation for the themes and objectives of this book.

Introduction 5

He was working at a hockey camp assisting a veteran coach with young players. The coach started the camp with the youngest novices, some standing on hockey skates for their first time, spread out over the ice, each with a puck and facing the same goal. He positioned himself in front of the net and being a "wide body" wearing hockey goalie equipment knew what they could and couldn't see from their location. He asked if anyone had a shot on goal, saw an opening into which to shoot the puck past him into the net. Predictably, each said no. He had them move locations on the ice, maneuvering their pucks as they would in a game, and when they settled in a new location, asked again. Again, predictably, each said no. So after each, from their various locations, declared what seemed as "true" to them, that there was no opening to shoot the puck past him and into the net, he had them change location one more time, but a change totally unlike the previous one. From where they stood he had each bend down on their knees, press their cheek against the cold ice, and look through the puck's "line of sight" towards the net, while he maintained the position he had taken all along. Then they saw what had previously been camouflaged, what had been unseen, invisible, declared before to be untrue. They saw all kinds of openings camouflaged while standing upright. "Becoming good at hockey," the coach said, "is learning to skate upright but play with the eyes of a puck."

It's a good story about both location and positionality. Location can be described simply as where you are, while positionality, to be taken up later, can be described as what view you take up from where you are.

So, to play hockey well you have to skate upright as fast as you can, dodging all kinds of seen challenges (and large bodies!) coming at you at breakneck speed, a constant and fluid change of locations. But to take a shot that might win a game, you must imaginatively calculate from a positionality. And as one of the greatest hockey players of all time reportedly said, "You miss 100% of the shots you don't take."[1] You have to choose a positionality from your current location to generate a new space for something more! You have to generate what philosophers call a "counterfactual . . . planning and anticipating our future states, and considering near and far alternatives to the actual state of the world."[2]

It begins with knowing your location as thoroughly as possible while maintaining the recognition that you can always grow in knowledge about where you are. It's the first step in becoming self-conscious: to realize you possess assumptions born of your context and shaping your point of view. Yet, one can too easily forget that every location camouflages so much! There is never a location that sees all paths into the hockey opponent's net any more than there is only your particular view that there simply isn't one there. Ask any hockey coach. Interpretation of any kind involves knowing location as a position circumscribing the sensations of the seen and

6 Introduction

unseen, sound and silence, speech and speechless, fragrance and odor, and the apparent and the camouflaged.

The concept of "location" is more than a passing interest in academia. One of religious studies' late 20th century contributions to the epistemological project that is the university, was adding its voice to the recognition that understanding of location is central to the scholar's task. Jonathan Z. Smith is routinely quoted identifying that, "Religion is solely the creation of the scholar's study. It is created for the scholar's analytic purposes by his imaginative acts of comparison and generalization."[3] Many religious studies scholars wrestle with the meaning of it for our field. For our purposes, though, it is a description of the context of the university, the location within which all scholars reside and out of which all scholarship emerges. For interdisciplinarians it is foremost about the need to be aware of location, and the manner in which one's point of view shapes and is shaped by the university location. The concepts any scholar uses in any discipline or field arise within the university. Specific to the field of the academic study of religion as interdisciplinary, to acknowledge location is a kind of rite of passage and today Smith's declaration is part of that rite.

Yet, he also continues that "the student of religion, and most particularly the historian of religion, must be relentlessly self-conscious. Indeed, this self-consciousness constitutes his [sic] primary expertise, his foremost object of study."[4] For the interdisciplinary religious studies scholar this self-consciousness is a necessary condition for performing interdisciplinarity. But the interpretive lens indicative of the interdisciplinary style of performing a methodology in any field is not pointed at that self-consciousness but rather is in part composed of that self-consciousness.

To be self-conscious of location is to develop an understanding of the multiplicities of location that influences one and be aware of the complexities of overlapping locations as a prelude to studying the activity of others. This is necessary because to study another is to interpret from the outside how an activity functions for those residing inside of that activity. And to know as thoroughly as possible the characteristics of one's location is the beginning of interdisciplinary study, though not an extensive description of it.

David Tracy identified the prevalence of interpretation in ways that encourage linking the scholar's task to self-conscious awareness so as to produce intentionality regarding location:

> Every time we act, deliberate, judge, understand, or even experience, we are interpreting. To understand at all is to interpret . . . Interpretation is thus a question as unavoidable, finally, as experience, understanding, deliberation, judgment, decision, and action.[5]

Self-consciousness regarding location has become a necessary prelude to the scholarly development of concepts and their use through methodologies suitable to a field or discipline. A scholar needs to know and disclose not only their locations, but the integration of all the locations that shape them, because every instance of observation and study is an interpretation that is complicit with location.

Moreover, David Tracy pointed out that, "Any act of interpretation involves at least three realities: some phenomenon to be interpreted, someone interpreting the phenomenon, and some interaction between the first two realities."[6] Interpretations are circumscribed by the location of whomever is performing the interpreting, and who bear preunderstandings brought to the action, decision, judgement, deliberation, understanding, or experience. Particular to each of us are "certain personal question, opinions, responses, expectations, even desires, fears and hopes . . . [which are] never merely personal and never simply static."[7] Locations yield preunderstandings borne by the scholar into every instance of interpretation and no one is exempt, least of all those who use evidence. I tell students in my "Religions of the World" class that we are not studying these traditions objectively (nor subjectively for that matter), but through preunderstandings we recognize and those uncovered during the formation of one's approach to study. This is both the foundation of interdisciplinarity and the continuous revealing involved in performing it. And lest one labor under the illusion that the scientist is an objective interpreter, those living in Michigan in the United States know the consequence of maintaining a hermeneutical illusion denying science's allegiance to funding, to political machinations, to past explanations, even to the primacy of science as the origin of the principles of organizing knowledge. That was one reason it took so long for the citizens of Michigan to learn about lead in the Flint city water when the scientific community was well aware long before any public acknowledgement![8] No one gathers evidence without preunderstandings derived from their context and absent unseen allegiances.

Whether in the setting of the university or any other setting, part of higher education is a deeper self-awareness of personal history and cultural design than what one has realized before, in order to study as thoroughly as possible activity involving others. Part of an interdisciplinarity style of performing methodology is a self-revealing-to-self. But that is a foundation and by-product of interdisciplinary study, not the object of it. One's vigorous pursuit of self-understanding forms is a necessary strategy not an endpoint, a trajectory in methodology not a target. In my previous location as a parish minister in a preaching tradition one would be absent self-consciousness were one to deny or disregard that the people addressed on Sunday morning put food on one's table on Monday. Yet as in my new location in the

8 *Introduction*

university, interpretation and understanding is and will be shaped by what the scholar sees and doesn't see, has been taught to see and not to see, and teaches others to see and not see. And at this time in the development of religious studies in the university a similar strategy is necessary.

In the academic study of religion our way is not the way of theology where the truth and meaning of the activity is prominent. Speaking as someone who has moved locations they are related but distinct; in a theological location the meaning of activity is prominently embedded in activity that "we" insiders perform as the depth of meaning is in doing the activity; whereas in a religious studies location the activity of "those" who are insiders is academically studied in terms of its function in order to achieve knowledge and understanding. Yet as religious studies has developed over the past three decades, the profession now considers much more deeply the formation of personal history and the influence of cultural architectural design on the scholar's point of view, and the self-consciousness in the academic study of religion has come to mirror more closely my previous professional location.

Also, while a Christian parish pulpit can be characterized as embodying meaning, that is not to insist that the scholar's study in a public university doesn't deal with truth and meaning. It's just that truth is not as prominent in the religious studies scholar's study in the same way that it is in the philosophy professor's study across the campus in the College of Liberal Arts and Sciences. And the philosophy professor studies truths, unlike the theologian who declares and is aligned and embedded – resides, in a word, inside and within certain truths in a tradition of truths. And, in my interdisciplinary college we do study semiotics, the study of meaning and how it's generated. But that is different than the theologian whose chief aim is to generate meaning in the activity the scholar produces, and the pulpit theologian who takes meaning and integrates it with certain actions and not others.

If we want or need to know the meaning or truth of an activity we will ask insiders, as the theologian, the pulpit theologian, the pew theologian, clergy and laity, or any other of a number of names and designations for the insiders who we study as scholars. And, as scholars we use that data only as it relates to how the activity functions for them. It is a difference in position to say, "We generate meaning and truth through our actions," as to say, "We generate knowledge about what we are studying, and what we do when we study and how best to study the actions of others." While they have common historical understandings we will illumine, the modern classroom is not to the scholar as the sacred space is to a practitioner. Or, to say it in a way that reveals personal history, studying college football and playing college football are different, even though persons for whom studying is prominent may play in a pickup game, and those who play for your university's team as a prominent activity may study an opponent's tendencies during the week.

Introduction 9

But one thing interdisciplinarity acknowledges is that in the university setting the specialization of knowledge and division organizationally into disciplines functions to imply boundaries. Yet, the interdisciplinary scholar realizes that "Boundaries . . . shift and overlap because ideas and techniques do not exist in a fixed place."[9] Thus, in an interdisciplinary style of methodological performance a concern for boundaries couples with the recognition that overlapping territories are characteristic of boundary and, hence, interdisciplinary work: "conflicting interpretations of the same phenomena, leads to boundary disputes."[10]

Looking at the same phenomenon, a Sikh in prayer for example, what is the boundary between questions asked in a philosophy and in a religious studies classroom? Here in my own location the Philosophy Department teaches a course called the "Philosophy of Religion," describing as any good university department should their location in the first sentence of the course description: "Does God exist?"[11] While we will here use philosophy to evaluate what concepts can and cannot do, how they can and cannot be used, this question we would not address in a normative way. Our way is not sociology, though the activity we will study has a social component in terms of identity. It is not psychology, though there is a component involving concepts of the self and of individual identity. Finally, it is not anthropology, as for us here religious activity, while a component of culture, generates an unseen order that comes out of culture but embodies for the insider an experience of something in addition to culture. Our interest here is in *how activity functions for insiders in this additional way*. The approach here welcomes the integration of the work of scholars in those disciplines, most especially philosophy and the social sciences because our field has a history of doing this. But, we occupy a different location, an interdisciplinary location in a field of study that may be looking at the same phenomenon as the others mentioned, but whose bounded territory involves an overlap of several of them.

This concern for boundaries and overlapping territory will be useful in terms of a key assumption in interdisciplinarity: "the reality beyond the academy requires an interdisciplinary approach to research and education"[12] because the aim of interdisciplinary scholarly preparation in the university is to point a constructed lens towards phenomena outside the university. However "religion" is defined, whatever is determined *by the scholar* to be "religious" activity distinct from, but including cultural activity, the one distinguishing factor for those located inside the phenomenon being studied, is that while to the outside observer they are observed in the profane, seen world, to them they occupy a sacred, unseen realm of time and place. Insiders reside in an overlapping boundary generated from cultural products and processes used in ways characteristic of sacrality. The observing scholar

10   *Introduction*

resides in only one of those domains producing that overlap. One cannot say the hockey players and the game's spectators are located in the same way relative to the activity. One is playing, the other is watching them play. But, as a spectator sport hockey involves both player and viewer. When the activity involves only players, one can call it a closed practice. When it involves only viewers, the pre-game. And sitting in the stands and skating on the ice are different locations, and those must be taken into account. The spectator who doesn't consider how the experience functions for those on the ice is the fan who may appreciate the game, but surely is not studying it. Study involves sympathetically inquiring about the activity in terms of the insider. In the academic study of religion that cannot involve asking what the activity means, explicitly, because study then becomes theological, or implicitly, which has occupied much of the field's self-examination over the last few decades. But sympathetic inquiry still needs to be initiated, and the most relevant form is seeking how the activity functions and what insiders know residing inside that activity as it is functioning, that outsiders do not.

Self-consciousness concerning location is just the beginning. Scholars hide their locations from themselves, maybe not intentionally, but by not considering the levels of location or by living during a time when those levels have yet to be understood or valued. Much of the necessary critique of Mircea Eliade characteristic of the latter 20th century resulted in an awareness of the need for additional self-consciousness of location. He was influenced by place, his Eastern European location, and time, the rise of Fascism, in ways that shaped his thinking unaware. Regardless of how his and others' ideas should be evaluated, his lack of discernment relative to his historical and cultural location colors his legacy and the formation of the concepts he constructed and used to interpret the activities of others. But his investment in the great project to create a science of religions also embodies his location in the modern university that privileges certain kinds of knowledge and organizes what it gathers in certain ways. It is part of the intellectual development of the academic study of religion that neglect of personal location is no longer responsible scholarship. What is the boundary between enthusiastic study of insider activity and allegiance to the insider residence being studied? Well, what is the boundary between disdain for the characteristics of certain insider activity and antagonism towards the insider residence being studied? Scholars in religious studies interpret the activities of others such that one could say we are interpreting the narrative lives and activities of others through our own narratives. To be self-conscious is to be aware of how personal and professional locations influence how we conceive and think how and as we do.

Religious studies then, has an additional layer to location that involves its historical development in the Western university and the scholar's presence

Introduction 11

in a location within that larger history. When stepping into a scholar's study in religious studies, one is stepping into a location with a lineage coinciding with the university's ancestry, and with personal preunderstandings already formed in a way that other scholars in other fields and disciplines may not. Additionally, the university was born as an educational product of medieval Christendom's theological vision, grew up as belief fortified by theology and the universality of "natural religion" appeared as separate and contesting, and entered adolescence with first the linguistic, then social scientific, then scientific, then social constructionist reconfiguring turn on "religion" while maintaining the split from theology and belief. As a location for epistemological production the university is already implicated and complicit in this field in ways no other academic field or discipline is; only science and philosophy come close but only as historical contenders. But no university discipline or field of study involves studying activity that formed the DNA of the university, nor finds itself more representative of the university and higher education's current identity crisis. Regardless of how or whether one interprets the university location of religious studies, a distinctive artifact of the historical founding and cultural development of the university as an epistemological location remains. And interdisciplinarity reveals how when the religious scholar steps into the study, the scholar is also bearing preunderstandings regarding the field of study in ways others in academia might not.

Could one imagine this question in a biomedical science class full of undergraduates seeking to become medical doctors, "Do you have to have had cancer to study cancer?" Or in legal studies, "Do you have to have had a run in with the law or been sued, to study law?" When asked or not asked, we know students are wondering, "Do you have to believe [*FILL IN THE BLANK*] to study religion?" and the more personal, "I bet the professor believes [*THUS AND SO*]," associating belief, as the integration of thought with will in actions that shape life purpose, or the lack of it with positionality in ways other disciplines and fields do not have to deal. Can I have been a parish minister in this culture and still teach and write in the academic study of religion? Can I be an atheist? Can I be a tribal elder, a yogi, or spiritual but not religious, and still teach and write in the academic study of religion? No other field or discipline in the university involves overlapping boundaries in this way. For the interdisciplinary religious studies scholar the answer is, it depends. It depends upon how personality and self-consciousness figure into positionality. But, that is a characteristic of interdisciplinarity.

In other words, what the critique of Eliade and the contribution of Smith confirm is that now to the modern religious studies scholar, self-consciousness must include intellectual self-critique as before but now also an understanding of how the location of self in many of its complexities and layers, composes a significant part of one's point of view. This development

12 *Introduction*

in the academic study of religion confirms the concept of self in William James and others, as being composed

> *In its widest possible sense . . . [as] the sum total of all that he* CAN *call his*, not only his body and his psychic powers, but his clothers and his house, his wife and children, his ancestors and friends, his reputation and works, his lands and horses, and yacht and bank-account.[13]

Personal history alone does not determine point of view but is basic to it. The moods, motivations, and manner of the scholar regarding what is studied and how are integral to the scholar's point of view. We might all assume all hockey players love their sport but that is mistaking location for positionality. They are related but distinct.

Understanding that distinction can help one become more self-conscious about the point of view one develops. And thus the interdisciplinarian in religious studies, who must consider location in its complexity, can find resources in sibling approaches that are shaped similarly by location. One sibling approach to interdisciplinary study is autoethnography, "a method of culling the researcher's own experiences in order to theorize larger phenomena."[14] While we might not use ethnography per se, we nevertheless need to scrutinize, understand, and develop an interpretive lens through our personal and professional location because as interdisciplinarians we know it will assuredly be evident in what we produce whether we are or are not self-conscious. The autoethnographer offers her own location in a way analogous to interdisciplinarity especially when using that style the field of religious studies: "Autoethnography . . . requires I lay bare my own life in a way that paints a muddy picture in order to reflect fully on the ways in which mothering, specifically noncustodial mothers, shapes my teaching identity and practice."[15]

Location and the self-conscious development of positionality by the interdisciplinary religious studies scholar

Religious studies, or the academic study of religion, is first a way to study human activity as religious in a way we, as students of these phenomena, deem them to be religious. We create the concepts and methods whereby we find certain human activity interesting and call it "religious," discarding other activity as not so much. As religious studies scholars, though, we do not create concepts *ex nihilo* but from a history of concept creation and use in the university, and mostly from other disciplinary locations, and through conversation and evaluation come to fashion them in a particular way as

Introduction 13

useful in understanding activity in a particular way. Other approaches to knowledge creation might use the same or similar concepts, but our aim is not that of the anthropologist, the philosopher, the psychologist, or even the theologian. Hockey is not the only sport that involves sticks shaped to hit objects, or skates and skating, or but the concept of "speed" and "hitting" function differently in the hockey player hitting an object (puck) with a stick while skating, than in baseball or cricket, or racing in long-track speed skating. The same activities are taught differently for different aims.

For this book we will choose a location – the academic study of religion called religious studies, a field within the modern university – that gives study a particular trajectory towards understanding how activities function religiously for insiders. While that might not be how other scholars would describe our location, this description is fitted to the purposes of the book by a scholar shaped by his positionality in an interdisciplinary college housing a religious studies program. In other words, in interdisciplinarity it is crucial for the scholar to address and understand positionality. For the interdisciplinary religious studies scholar, standing as we do in an academic location with the particular history of the epistemological development of the university religious studies carries, and bring to that academic location moods and motivations, the manner in a word regarding what we are studying, how we are positioned to study is critical to acknowledge and embrace. It involves a rigor distinctive to religious studies.

With an epistemic aim location can be called "situatedness," because "all aspects of the production of knowledge are situated."[16] Truth comes from knowledge and knowledge is produced in a situation, from a location. Claims that there is a form of knowledge that is objective is claiming that located nowhere you can claim to be everywhere. Making truths subjective is no better, you have your truth and I have mine, the claim "of being somewhere while claiming to be everywhere equally."[17] Both deny the human contribution to what we call truth, deny that we have a location, are situated somewhere. Young hockey players at the beginning of camp assure the coach that there are no openings to shoot the puck into! The coach then teaches them how to shoot the puck amidst situatedness.

Knowing where one is located fosters knowing your identity, and knowing where and how one is situated is an additional piece of self-knowledge. Situatedness is part of recognizing that embodiment characterizes human knowing, and that often when scholars forget or neglect this they are in denial about their personal attachment to what they are studying; that is, the moods and motivations guiding a relationship to what is coming *to be known in a particular way*. While using ethnography directly is only a particular methodological form in our field, autoethnography describes ethnology in terms of the nature of the embodied self-as-scholar involved in the

14   *Introduction*

epistemic process, and does so in ways that are helpful to the distinctive situatedness of the interdisciplinary religious studies scholar who brings particular preunderstandings regarding the phenomena of interest that are peculiar to our field:

> like ethnographers, autoethnographers attempt to achieve cultural understanding through analysis and interpretation. In other words, autoethnography is not about focusing on self alone, but about searching for understanding of others (culture/society) through self . . . The last aspect of autoethnography sets it apart from other ethnographic inquiries. Autoethnographers use their personal experiences as primary data.[18]

While unlike autoethnographers we may not always use our personal experiences as primary data, the distinctive nature of our inquiry means they are never far from the surface. Otherwise, the critical analysis of Eliade and others regarding political and cultural location would constitute an inappropriate link between the personal and the professional. Or, the question of whether an atheist can teach the academic study of religion is irrelevant and inconsequential. And, we should rebuke students who ask us whether we are located in a particular religious tradition as an affront. Situatedness matters and so do the moods and motivations of the scholar and the university context within which scholars reside, because that's a deep part of what we bring to the epistemic process we are involved in. "We are . . . resident on earth . . . [yet] this is not a merely empirical characterization of us . . . [but] a deep and necessary feature of our being."[19]

Knowing self-identity as comprehensively as possible in the moment is a prelude to the scholar's enterprise. None can proffer a position out of the field of religious studies regarding the interpretation or meaning of a phenomenon as religious, without the self-identification involved in location. Scholars generate knowledge from a location, the scholar's study,[20] but as part of a process that involves multiple locations, all of which are resided in at various times in that process. And each instance of residing holds different qualities of situatedness: *the university before* heading out to engage *the activity of insiders in the field* only to *return to the scholar's study in the university* to evaluate and generate formally a contribution of knowledge. Of course, observation and knowing and knowledge production goes on in all three of these locations, but the crucial contribution of interdisciplinarity is the identification of these as three different situations and that the *return* from outside to inside involves a different aim than disciplinary ones.

Thus, when the scholar engages in activity outside the university as observer to insiders residing in an overlapping domain constructed as sacred

Introduction 15

for insider residence and the recognitions embodied there, observing scholars inhabit a space in-between outsider and insider, a scholar's liminal. As a new space it is a unique positionality. This space is neither the scholar's study where concepts were initially generated in conversations in the academic study of religion within the university as an epistemological project and from which the scholar has separated, nor the space of insiders whose actions generate residence within a sacred unseen order they know and are known by. It's also not the space the interdisciplinary scholar has predicted with concepts formed in the previous university location, nor the anticipated new space of knowledge formation upon return to the university. The manner in which scholars take residence in the scholar's liminal bears their bias. A faculty colleague in paleontology and geology might hold to his claim of a "no bias" positionality while teaching that an asteroid impact caused the dinosaurs' extinction, but interdisciplinary religious studies scholars cannot maintain the same position. As soon as the religious studies scholar steps into interdisciplinarity an epistemological critique of the historical and cultural location of the university begins as a part of self-consciousness. For example, identifying the political nature of language is one such component of the university's location in the current era. So also does critique of the scholar's own location and its influence on positionality form part of the scholar's self-consciousness. If the positions the religious studies scholar wrestles with in the university become the box to fit within the insider's activities outside the university, no new space is generated and interdisciplinary has been abandoned.

In most of the university the performance of knowledge production when returning from the outside is a disciplinary approach defined as "sets of problems, methods, and research practices or as bodies of knowledge . . . [and] social [and professional] networks of individuals interested in related problems or ideas."[21] Disciplinary formation is the result and accelerant of increased specialization in knowledge gathering. It breeds what interdisciplinarity calls knowledge silos with characteristics carried throughout the university. The positionality developed in any university location is influenced by this increased specialization. And so is the expectation that knowledge be organized by scientific principles that assume a distance from what is studied that our field struggles with because of the tension between our situatedness in the university and our personal situatedness in the field we are in. A scientist can lift a human cell out of the body, place it between two microscopic plates, and observe it under a microscope. But, it is not the cell inside the scholar's body. There are things learned this way, of course. But when taken to activities outside the university location where they were formed, concepts and methods are transformed and change what knowledge would be formed where they confined in their utilization to the university

16   *Introduction*

location alone. In religious studies debating concepts at a scholar's brown bag roundtable is not test driving them on the road.

Part of the lineage of Enlightenment historicity has been to analyze and bring forward the way the Enlightenment conceived of "religion" as "faith against reason" – to which "religion" eagerly contended and eventually accepted. The academic study of religion maintained the objective-subjective split of the Enlightenment, and when pushed in the academy to justify itself in the 20th century, invented the History of Religions as the project that would fulfill the scientific objectivity the Enlightenment required for knowledge to be housed in the university. As a part of research and knowledge formation we recollect that history as part of critique, but what is done by the scholar with the bias more than dealing with it in the academic study of religion?; and, in the university's hallways where science relegates religion to "faith" as the foe of science?; and on a campus filled with students who have been shaped by a culture that fetishizes costs of education and living and getting a job?

In the academic study of religion the limits of the modern university as an epistemological project have been known for some time, though it was stated as a disappointment attributable to the study of religion rather than as a critique of the university location as it performs its purpose in the modern age. In a 1970 collection of essays edited by Paul Ramsey and John F. Wilson, compiled mostly from addresses given at a conference honoring George F. Thomas, the first unit head for Princeton University's Religion Department established in 1946, 20th-century luminaries like Krister Stendahl, William Clebsch, Jacob Neusner, and James Gustafson among others assessed the academic study of religion or, as many called it then, the History of Religions. Though not in its infancy, it was still seeking to differentiate itself from theology, philosophy, and the social sciences, as justifying a different and new location in the university. Scholars sought to justify it as a distinct discipline that could operate as a science. In a contribution entitled, "The History of Religions: Some Problems and Prospects," H. P. Sullivan of Vassar College wrote:

> It would be naïve to suppose – and some historians of religions have been guilty of so supposing – that objectivity or purely "scientific" examination is possible in describing and interpreting religious phenomena. No matter how intellectually cognizant one is of one's own religious position, there still remains the subtle play of emotions and temperament on one's perspective and understanding. But not just irrational or nonrational factors may intrude. For there are also the effects of some basic philosophical suppositions to take into account – not simply personal ones, but those of one's culture . . . Especially prominent

Introduction 17

today is the awareness that the questions which the history of religions has been posing and the categories it has been employing are largely Western ones, conditioned by Western concepts of man and religion.[22]

In this earlier recognition of self-conscious location one can see issues of positionality being foreshadowed: the reconsideration of its most basic concepts including the "sacred and profane," theories like the "religious and secular opposition," and even the concept of "religion" itself; the relationship between the possible religious allegiances of the scholar and its ramifications when studying a religious "other," especially the theological problem, the problem of location in relation to positionality, and whether a "science" is feasible and if not, what prospects there might be within the location of the university. If the study of religion cannot conform to the ordering principles of science, does it have a future in the university?

What is omitted is telling. There is no historicizing lens turned towards the modern university as an epistemological project within which religious studies emerged to understand itself in a particular way. Nothing about how in not conforming to the ordering principles of science, religious studies might just be contesting the narrow epistemic viewpoint of modernism and the university. Nothing about the origin of the university in medieval Christendom and the ramifications of that for the future trajectory of this unique process of knowledge production. Tracing the history of the intellectual and epistemological development of the context through a critique of that development was lacking. Interdisciplinarity is a style of producing knowledge that embodies this critique.

It's common in classes to ask first-year religious studies students if one needs to "have a religion" to study religious activity, and another but different question concerning one's beliefs about god(s). I would argue that because of the nature of the activity that we study and where we study it – that is, positionality in religious studies – the foundation of personal assumptions and historical preunderstandings forming cultural context integrate in the question. And the question needs to be engaged before going outside the university to study human activity framed by the academic study of religion. The question forms a way to address the manner of studying "how to study" in the university location, in order to use that to study activity outside the university. It is the foundation of understanding positionality as informed by but separate than location. It permits the discussion of relationship to the phenomenon as something more than "I am part of it in a particular way" or "I am not a part of it in a particular way." It invites transition to analogy, as in, "What is the relationship between a medical doctor's mental and physical health, and studying medicine, and practicing medicine?" It becomes a foundation for separating study and practice,

18 *Introduction*

discussing how that separation is constructed and is useful and not, and how the idea of something being "prominent" doesn't exclude other activities. In other words, it is the foundation for an interdisciplinary style of performing research. As interdisciplinary religious studies scholar students we are studying study as a practice, in order to study those who practice and study their practice; however in each location the positionality of study/practice includes different ideas as to what constitutes each as an activity and how that activity functions for insiders who hold study as prominent, and others who hold practice as prominent.

These questions forming the foundation of positionality are a prelude to the classroom practice of each student posting their definitions of religion as a transition to discussing historical assumptions and cultural preunderstandings embedded in their definitions. And, thus, a critique of the origin and development of the concept of religion.

The form and structure of the book

The structure of this book can be easily summarized. Overall, it presents a description of the location and situatedness of the scholar adopting an interdisciplinary positionality for knowledge production in religious studies. The epistemic process identified in interdisciplinarity begins with the location and situatedness of the scholar in the university, moves outside that location to the engagement of an activity involving a different location and situatedness, to return to the university to engage directly in a new form of situatedness shaped by the interdisciplinary knowledge production process. The integration involved in the process forms the positionality of the interdisciplinary religious studies scholar.

This introduction has set the foundation for forming the positionality of the interdisciplinary religious studies scholar. Chapter One presents the historical development of the university and the study of religion in the university as viewed through an interdisciplinary critique. It locates the university as an epistemological project and situates religious studies as residing there. The university will be presented as an epistemological project designed to gather and order information, with disciplinary structure as the means for gathering and producing knowledge and the library as the institutional repository and symbol for storing and disseminating knowledge. During different historical eras this context has valued certain kinds of knowledge production by gathering and ordering techniques guided by central evaluating principles originating initially in the theology of medieval Christendom, to be supplanted by philosophy in the Reformation and Enlightenment, to reside today in modern science in the form of scientism. The study of religion – what activity that was referring to, how it was categorized and

Introduction   19

understood, and how that study was conducted – has been shaped by each as epistemological organizing principles for the university during the eras when one held sway over the other two. Two recent features have emerged to indicate that the central evaluating principle is shifting towards something new: first, the university's chief ordering structure both literally and symbolically, the library, has been usurped in its traditional role by the computer age's easy access to stored knowledge. In the laptop and tablet the student holds more capacity to access stored information than the bookshelves of nearly all university libraries combined. And secondly, within religious studies there have been efforts to move beyond how social constructionist critiques, rooted in science and political philosophy, changed the central 20th-century effort to produce a science of religions. The practice of interdisciplinarity is evident in these arenas of study among others: Material Religion, Religion and Film Studies, Religion and the Body, and studies employing the Participatory Turn. To identify the characteristics of interdisciplinarity in these efforts can help in developing a conceptual foundation for an interdisciplinary positionality in religious studies in addressing a social question, "How does religious activity function for insiders?" While that is not the only question coming out of religious studies, it is a product of a positionality in religious studies that is favorable for retooling concepts for interdisciplinary use.

With an interdisciplinary foundation laid for retooling concepts in religious studies, Chapter Two begins that process with the basic concept that is taken from the university outside in an encounter with activity, the sacred/ profane. Vis-à-vis interdisciplinary critique, that concept will be historicized in the university context in chronicling the origin of it in the university location as the sacred and secular, maintained in the social scientific binary of two domains – the sacred and the profane, which was until recently conflated into one cultural domain by some, the profane. What will emerge is that both the romanticism of the 19th- and 20th-century developments in the academic study of religion, and the social constructionist critiques unto our own day, participate in a kind of reductionism that has flattened the use of the concept. Interdisciplinarity forges a different path, the creation of a new space for knowledge, and we'll use philosophical New Realism to help clear that path, which we'll call insiders residing in an overlapping domain, the sacred-profane, while simultaneously sharing residence with the scholar in the profane. Simultaneity as characteristic of insider residence will be the foundation of this newly created space, the overlapping domain of the sacred-profane.

The third chapter involving concepts in religious studies also forms the novel creation of an interdisciplinary foundation in religious studies through the retooling of a concept that hitherto has been on the periphery

20   *Introduction*

of the field. In his 1901–1902 Gifford Lectures, later to become the classic *The Varieties of Religious Experience*, William James introduced a concept that gained little traction in the nearly century and a quarter since: the unseen order. As the interdisciplinary foundation for the study of religion has developed in this book, it involves a turn towards the function of insider experience while residing in the overlapping domains of the sacred-profane as the scholar can observe them. One chief result of the activity of residing in that overlapping domain is the way that knowledge formation by insiders both mimics knowledge produced in the profane domain shared with the observing scholar, as well as an additional effect. This is a product of insiders' residence generating a sacred, unseen order and the subsequent residing in that unseen order while to the scholar simultaneously residing in the profane domain shared with the scholar. We'll evaluate "residing" in any domain as the combination of two concepts, sense of presence and immersion, both from the academic study of virtual reality environments (VREs) as generating an overlapping domain with the room where subjects are experiencing the VREs while being monitored by researchers. This technological advance invites us to conceive of studying the religious activity of insiders in this new way. Tracing the epistemological development of the religious studies concept within the context of the university, as interdisciplinarity does, allows a retooling of that concept in the context of new technological developments and what they tell us about the effects of human activity.

The next effort at retooling basic concepts in religious studies for use in the 21st century will be the fourth chapter's treatment of the Eliadian concept of the hierophany as a concept describing the effect of residing in the sacred-profane unseen order in terms of processes, persons, objects, and events engaged in by insiders within the overlapping sacred-profane domain. Observing religious activity involves scholars assessing the function of insider activities and objects rather than the meaning of insider involvement in them, rightfully the domain of theology, justification by insiders. Part of studying this function in the interdisciplinary way we are developing involves the movements of insiders within an overlapping domain made up by residing simultaneously in a sacred, unseen order and a seen profane one. As time and place are foundational characteristics of domains and the way human beings order them and, hence, reside inside of them, this will be explored. A foundation for understanding the implications of insider residence upon activities involving objects and processes, etc., will be developed using a framework constructed by the phenomenology of embodiment by Maurice Merleau-Ponty.

The final chapter serves to summarize the argument of the book and the interdisciplinary foundation the book has set forth for the reprising and

Introduction 21

retooling of basic concepts for use in religious studies. It recaps the characteristics of interdisciplinarity and its use in religious studies.

Finally, like all persons, part of my location and situatedness today and, hence, my positionality is shaped by yesterday. I was born and raised in an Indiana environment that once would be called "unchurched." I graduated from a Presbyterian college that, quite frankly, I attended in order to play football. I found there what emerged and is still emerging as a lifelong pursuit: the drive to know and understand human being, being religious. It took me to the University of Chicago where I studied with David Tracy, Langdon Gilkey, Don Browning, Martin Marty, and sat in on the classes of Mircea Eliade, unaware then of the deep influence all would have on me. I also took a doctorate from the Unitarian Universalist theological school, Meadville Lombard, where I prepared for the 27 years I spent in parish ministry. I was trained in the academic study of religion and spent a large part of my life in the practice of a particular kind in a particular tradition in a particular culture. My situatedness and positionality were different there and then, and I used what I knew and what I sought to know differently. I returned to the study of religion when I transitioned into my current location, Grand Valley State University, a public university in Michigan, and onto the faculty in the newly formed Religious Studies Program in the Brooks College of Interdisciplinary Studies. All of those coordinates to my current location are critical to where I am on the ice, situated as I am in the hockey rink. When my skating brought me to my current location and I looked at the goal, I saw that the field was still largely looking at itself like a hockey player possessing the puck and in position to shoot but checking equipment instead of estimating the trajectory and taking a shot on goal. We continue analyzing our field as we should, but do so while people are engaged in activities needing our attentiveness in the way that we do. We are needed to take a shot on goal and help our cultures and times understand what is shaping it as much as anything else. This book is my first measured shot, hopefully not my last, but all mine. I had excellent mentors and supporters, so the misfires are all mine.

Notes

1 But even the origin of this quote depends upon location. It is attributed to Wayne Gretsky, who attributes a variation to his father Walter. Other variations are reported to have older origins in other sports. Retrieved at: www.barrypopik.com/index.php/new_york_city/entry/you_miss_100_of_the_shots_you_dont_take_hockey_adage

2 Caren Walker and Alison Gopnick, "Causality and Imagination."

3 Jonathan Z. Smith, 1982, p. xi.

4 Ibid.

5 David Tracy, *Plurality and Ambiguity*, p. 9.

6 Ibid., p. 10.

22   *Introduction*

7 David Tracy, *The Analogical Imagination*, p. 118.
8 Steve Kolowich, "The Water Next Time: Professor Who Helped Expose Crisis in Flint Says Public Science Is Broken."
9 Julie Thompson Klein, 1996, p. 43.
10 Ibid., p. 70.
11 The full description reads, "Does God exist? Is there a life after death? How did evil enter the world? Is there any place for reason in religion, or is religious faith only a matter of subjective experience? Questions like these will be considered, as well as the answers that have been given to them by some important religious philosophers." Retrieved at: www.gvsu.edu/philosophy/course-offerings-18.htm
12 Allen F. Repko, 2012, p. 52.
13 William James, 1950 edition, p. 291.
14 Marilyn Preston, 2018, p. 1.
15 Ibid.
16 Ericka Engelstad and Siri Gerrard, 2005, pp. 1–6.
17 Ibid.
18 H. Chang, 2008, pp. 48–49 as quoted in Boylorn and Orbe, editors, 2014, p. 17.
19 David Morris, 2004, p. 131.
20 "If we have understood the archaeological and textual record correctly, man [sic] has had his entire history in which to imagine deities and modes of interaction with them. But man, more precisely Western man [sic], has had only the last few centuries in which to imagine religion. It is this act of second order, reflective imagination which must be the central preoccupation of any student of religion . . . Religion is solely the creation of the scholar's study. It is created for the scholar's analytical purposes by his [sic] imaginative acts of comparison and generalization. Religion has no independent existence apart from the academy. For this reason, the student of religion, and most particularly the historian of religion, must be relentlessly self-conscious. Indeed, this self-consciousness constitutes his primary expertise, his foremost object of study" (Jonathan Z. Smith, 1982, p. xi).
21 Lisa R. Lattuca, 2001, p. 23. Print.
22 H. P. Sullivan, 1970, pp. 251–252.

1 Locating the academic study of religion

An interdisciplinary critique of the epistemological development of the university

In 2010 I made the professional move from the sanctuary to the classroom. Graduate school prepared me both for a 27-year stint as a parish minister and also a current appointment onto the faculty of Grand Valley State University (GVSU), a 25,000-student public university in Michigan. GVSU was in the final stages of creating a religious studies major and minor.

The program would be housed in the Liberal Studies Department of the university's Brooks College of Interdisciplinary Studies, where it still resides. That is significant relative to academic identity. The academic study of religion was being conceived not as part of the College of Liberal Arts and Sciences, housing the Philosophy Department and all of the social sciences. It was installed in interdisciplinarity and has become an integral part of a department whose purpose involves advocating for and fulfilling the university's mission in liberal education. Location shapes purpose both institutionally and professionally.

In my first year I was privy to deliberations on the creation of this new program as in Faculty Senate meetings questions arose from various academic departments concerning the place in a public university for the study of religion. The epistemological privileging consistent with the historical development of the university location was on full display, and appropriately so. If a new academic major and minor was proposed it should be evaluated by the epistemological criterion represented in the location and as a means to fulfill the location's purpose. The questions could be categorized by issues reflecting more the culture's understanding of the concept of "religion," such as "church and state," and/or the distinction between theological study and religious practice, and theological study and religious studies: "Whose religion are we going to be teaching?" "Are we going to be interfaith?" "How can a public university teach religion?" Others, though, could be categorized by the discipline and specialty of the inquiring scholar with university structures: "Can/must I be a believer/atheist to teach religion?" "Are you going to teach world religions, employing a Rabbi to teach

24 *Locating the academic study of religion*

Judaism, a Muslim teaching Islam, etc.?" "How can a university that takes scientific method seriously, teach about faiths?" and of course, "What kinds of jobs will they be prepared for?" This category of question seemed more localized and curious to a newcomer. Even after establishing the program in 2012 and hiring faculty in the field of religious studies, questions continue to this day from faculty surprised to discover our university has a religious studies major and minor, and students who don't know the difference between it and theology.

This simply mimics the way our culture considers religion as involving faith, belief, and largely, the assumptions about what to look for when studying faiths other than Christian. And it adds a crucial something more: how being inside the university's structures of organizing compounds that complexity. But realizing the inescapable complexities involved when anyone studies the "religious inside" of another is part of the historical construction of the religious studies scholar's self-consciousness: "Thus, broadly speaking, information about religions may be transmitted through four channels: (1) insider-to-insider, (2) insider-to-outsider, (3) outsider-to-outsider, and (4) outsider-to-insider."[1] To those, one could add other domains that aren't as distinct, are more overlapping and fluid than four, like teaching weekdays in the university's Biology Department and on Sundays the Adam and Eve story in a Protestant Christian Sunday school. Regardless of the academic level, every class of mine must begin with a two-week introduction of the academic study of religion, its distinctions from theology, philosophy, and the social sciences, and how it is a different way to learn about this human activity than how it would be learned in a church, temple, or masjid. Because of multiple complexities, the concept of insider/outsider, and the prospect that some domains referred to by them are fluid and overlapping, is part of the student's orientation to the field. To be a self-conscious scholar involves among other things a knowledge of the history of a location and the language common to that location. And to be self-conscious in religious studies is to pursue that study as a dialogic endeavor involving one's positionality engaging others' positionalities.

This echoes my training in the early 1980s. One of my most exciting graduate experiences was a class on Darwin and evolution that mixed students from the divinity school, zoology, biology, history, and social sciences. The central challenge I thought was developing a common "class language" out of various academic locations; or, as was practiced, to ask a question and check responses from multiple academic locations. It embodied David Tracy's insight regarding communication, location, and hermeneutics: "Anyone who uses a language bears the preunderstandings, partly conscious, more often preconscious, of the traditions of that language."[2]

Locating the academic study of religion 25

Over 37 years and a change of professional locations, I understand Tracy's comment more deeply. Creating a common language might suggest that differences weren't somehow real, although it would propose what science might call an objective referent and suggest an object of study. And addressing a single question from multiple perspectives is indicative of performing multidisciplinarity, "an approach that juxtaposes disciplines . . . foster[ing] wider knowledge, information, and methods . . . [whereas the] integration of disciplines [is] the 'litmus test' of interdisicplinarity."[3] A multidisciplinary approach was what we had the first day in that Darwin class and that seemed to fragment knowledge into isolated towers. Tracy's observation now points me instead towards a different style of producing knowledge called interdisciplinarity.

If we are pursuing an understanding of what religious studies involves when it is performing interdisciplinarity, then first we need to describe what interdisciplinarity is and isn't. Secondly, we need to enumerate the foundational characteristics of interdisciplinarity as they pertain to religious studies and perform the central, foundational characteristic, the construction of

> a "parallax view" of intellectual history, whereby the normal account by which disciplines develop and give rise to interdisciplinary inquiry is taken to be only part of the whole story. There is at least one other side, which reflects a different sense of how things came to be as they are and how they might turn out to be in the future . . . [a kind of] counterfactual history.[4]

After establishing foundational characterisics we need to add secondary ones that form a cluster to distinguish an interdisciplinary style of performing methodology from others. And finally, we need to place the academic study of religion inside the domain of the university location as interdisciplinarity conceives of it and religious studies performs within it. This last aim will be begun in this chapter and continued throughout the rest of the book.

What does being "interdisciplinary" mean?

Interdisciplinarity is not a particular method of conducting study, not a methodology but a way to perform a given methodology. If methodologies – like comparison, explanation, description, and hermeneutics, commonly used in religious studies – were genres of music, interdisciplinarity would be a style within a genre. Mozart and Bach embody different styles within the genre of classical music, as do the Beatles and Santana in rock 'n roll, and Getz and Holiday in blues. As a performing style interdisciplinarity

26 *Locating the academic study of religion*

integrates disciplinary yields, and using intellectual rigor, pushes beyond the rigidity disciplines incline towards, to create a new space within which to generate knowledge.

Like the concept of "religion," interdisciplinarity is more amenable to a cluster description than a single definition. The Association for Interdisciplinary Studies – the professional organization for interdisciplinary practitioners – identifies interdisciplinarity as integrating "the insights of knowledge domains to produce a more comprehensive understanding of complex problems, issues, or questions [drawn from] real world applications."[5] Key to its style of methodological performance is an integrating trajectory aimed at understanding a first-order experience outside of the university. Self-conscious of three locations and the positionality created in each, the interdisciplinary scholar takes concepts formed in the university location into a positionality, brings that to a location outside the university to engage the activity forming phenomena in that context, and then back into the university for transforming that encounter into knowledge. Intrinsic to knowledge created through interdisciplinarity is a critique of all locations involved.

Scholars like Joe Moran[6] and Julie Thompson Klein[7] chronicle the dynamic relationship between the emergence of interdisciplinarity and its university location where scholarship begins. Today it critiques the historical/cultural development of the university's epistemological structure of separate disciplines. Producing knowledge through the techniques of its performance style it generates a liminal region where new knowledge can be generated, by "establishing a kind of undisciplined space in the interstices between disciplines, or even attempting to transcend disciplinary boundaries altogether."[8] Thus, interdisciplinarity counters the modern university form of gathering knowledge into disciplinary "silos" scientifically organized and governed, though by using disciplinary yields in a different way and not by rejecting them. This in turn impacts how knowledge is gathered, especially in terms of the specialization disciplinary knowledge favors, and the reductionism that specialization can lean into and towards. Interdisciplinarity employs a comprehensive critique of location to spawn new knowledge production.

The university is a location of language and thinking accumulated over centuries and shaped by various cultures into a project involving why people question what they do in the way in which they do, as well as where, when, and how they question. Therefore, interdisciplinarity represents epistemology as dialogic. History involves chronicling how time and place influence how something has come to be what it is considered to be. It locates. Thus, a foundational characteristic of interdisciplinarity is that it is a dialogic endeavor on the history of knowledge formation in the university location. In this sense, this chapter offers a view of how the study of religion emerged

Locating the academic study of religion 27

in the Western university. Obviously, it will be a condensed narrative told from a point of view, and offered by an individual who is, for better and worse, constructing this narrative in a way that involves a personal history interfacing with this culture at this time. Because of its unique embodiment of insider/outsider issues in the location of the university, religious studies performed as an interdisciplinary endeavor necessarily involves characteristics of an autoethnographic performance. "Autoethnography is a method of culling the researcher's own experiences in order to theorize larger phenomena"[9] by using the scholar's "personal experiences as primary data"[10] instead of disregarding it, and thus self-consciously using the field to construct the nature of the distance between scholarly study and practitioner activity.

The academic study of religion arose and developed within the intellectual forces of the university, as well as the lines of inquiry and allegiances to certain discourses and ways of organizing knowledge that are characteristic of it, at certain times and in certain places. How is it that the epistemological project that is the modern university developed in such a way that the study of religion within its walls is conducted and understood now in the way that it is?

The development of the university as an epistemological project: a creation narrative

To practice interdisciplinarity, the religious studies scholar needs to account for location personally and professionally, and basic to professional identity is location in the university as an epistemological project. It is the purpose of the university to produce knowledge, and to fulfill its aim functions to gather, organize, and disseminate what it produces. "Disciplinary development was meant to occur within the overall framework of the university as a community of essentially like-minded scholars: indeed, the term 'university' derives from the Latin, *universitas*, meaning 'universal' or 'whole.'"[11] Symbolic of its knowledge-gathering function are the scholar's study and the disciplinary department's hallways. Symbolic of the organizing function is the university library where the yields of the disciplines are housed in an ordered and unified way. It's to be noted and analyzed elsewhere that we have yet to see the full effect of students walking into university libraries carrying under their arms laptops that organize exponentially more information than any one library could ever house. And the disseminating function is represented by the classroom, which through the internet now expands well beyond physical hallways!

When Alfred North Whitehead identified the "Reason of Plato . . . [to be] in formulating judgments of the understanding"[12] of a whole he was both reflecting his location in history and culture, and raising up the role the

28 *Locating the academic study of religion*

Western university had institutionalized for philosophy: that of serving as an organizing principle tying the disparities of knowledge production into a unitary whole. In the West philosophy is rooted in "the attempt to make manifest the fundamental evidence as to the nature of things,"[13] and is driven by the prompts of consciousness as "two factors, interest and discrimination, stimulate each other."[14] In any given age it generates a "universal field of inquiry which brought together all the different branches of learning, a notion of unity in difference which also influenced the formation of the disciplines within the modern university."[15]

But in terms of the Western university there have been three lines of inquiry that have served this organizing function, each gaining prominence in an era over the other two. In addition to philosophy, religion and science have also wielded organizing power and thereby generated a contest amongst the three as to which would gain prominence as a chief epistemic unifier. While philosophy lays claim to a universal field of inquiry, so do religion and science, though Whitehead noted they function differently as organizers than philosophy and more closely mirror one other. For religion in the West, specifically Christianity, the foundation of its epistemology is in the movement from religious experience to formulation: "The dogmas of religion are the attempts to formulate in precise terms the truths disclosed in the religious experience of mankind."[16] And science operates intellectually "in exactly the same way [in that] the dogmas of physical science are the attempts to formulate in precise terms the truths disclosed in the sense-perception of mankind."[17] In other words, in the West and embedded in the structural foundation of both religion and science as a means of knowing, is the movement from experience to formulation; in religion, from experience/encounter with God to creedal formulation and orthodoxy, while in science, from the sense-perception experience/encounter with nature to hypothesis and theory. And unlike philosophy, the formulation generated by each harbors an exclusiveness regarding the world it creates in relation to the other and to philosophy. This holds certain consequences when evidenced in the location of the university.

When considering the university's unitary epistemological function, both involve a metaphysic. Science in the West creates one while Christianity searches for one. And operating as a metaphysic and as the university's organizing and ordering principles in a given era, both operate within the assumption that the knowledge gathered in the university forms the world as it is. Historically, it was initially Christianity that fulfilled the unitary function of epistemology, followed by Enlightenment philosophy, until today where the organizing principles are rooted in empirical science. In each era the primary organizing principles shaped how the other two were conceived of and performed in producing epistemological outcomes. In this way, and

Locating the academic study of religion 29

more to our interest here, "[i]nterdisciplinary study within the humanities is often an attempt to challenge the pre-eminence of the sciences as a model for disciplinary developments,"[18] especially as from the early 1800s on science was increasingly "to be distinguished clearly from philosophy in both academic and general usage."[19] It was science in its capacity as the ordering, unitary epistemological function of the university that influenced directly the nature of the discourse when the GVSU Faculty Senate was considering creating our religious studies program. It has been the organizing principles of the university in the modern era that, more than anything else, have given shape and substance to the disciplines and in the academic study of religion, to concepts like "religion," "world religions," "belief," and "secular" and "profane" and their critiques. It's what interdisciplinary critique uncovers and is the context in which interdisciplinary performance is situated.

From its beginnings the European university has consistently displayed two epistemological inclinations in its intellectual development that influence the historical view formulated below. First, the function of gathering the yield of observations of the natural world has maintained a gradual arc towards privileging increased specialization and detail. Humanity's epistemological inclinations include the desire to know the parts of its universe in their various particularities and the university mirrors this inclination. Secondly, the epistemological activity of reflecting upon the details has led to the weaving of those parts into an understandable whole, a process governed by particular principles for organizing knowledge. Through reflection humanity seeks to make sense of the "body of knowledge" it gathers, as an understandable whole organized into a unitary view. It became the university's role to posit, justify, and then safeguard the way the parts of knowledge gathered, make a comprehensible, organized "unitary whole," the "world" as it is known. The former is knowledge gathered and ordered today into specializations, the disciplines, as the gathering structure most suitable to the modern university's organizing principles in science. But in order for the gathering not to fragment into unrelated detail, the organizing function has gained in importance and consolidated its effect. The Western concepts of "religion" (variously understood differently in different eras), "philosophy," and "science" have continuously contested for leadership as the chief knowledge-ordering function in the university, which obviously shaped what was gathered and how, as well as the ways it was disseminated as knowledge. Each gained prominence in an era and shaped how scholars in the other two understood and performed their epistemic tasks.

It is within this epistemological context and culture that discourses and lines of inquiry still develop and are deemed by academics to be of interest or not, including the study of religion. Allegiances form in disciplinary departments, through personnel committee decision-making, collegial

30 Locating the academic study of religion

organizations, academic conferences, in all the various facets of professionalism. They're shaped by lawmakers and which economic forecasters are holding sway at any given time. Allegiances also form as lines of intellectual inquiry are deemed as interesting, and these allegiances can be traced back along the lines of inquiry to rest in disciplinary concepts and methodologies, shaped as they are by the university's unitary organizing principles.

The structure of the modern Western university as an epistemological project commenced in Europe in the 11th century with its development rooted in the Christian Church's organizational forms.[20] The university grew out of the earlier educational forms of scholastic guilds and before that, individual teachers. And while arguments can be made that the form of the modern university has many places of origin – Bologna, Oxford, Cambridge, Naples, Toulouse – "the decisive step in its development came when masters and scholars of various subjects and with diverse professional objectives first joined together to form a single guild or community"[21] in Paris. This form embodied something more and different than the previous forms of instruction by seeking "the ideal of making the teaching body representative of the whole cycle of human knowledge."[22]

Organizationally it developed as a part of Church bureaucracy as an extension of Church culture. The *universitas* promulgated the Christian Church's integrated view of existence and the knowledge yielded by experience, "the great medieval vision of the essential unity of church and state, with individual monarchs ruling their territories, all presided over by the pope."[23] But it was distinctive in three ways. As a structure within the medieval vision of unity, it maintained "a significant degree of legal autonomy and the right of self-governance, [in that] the corporation exercised control over its membership and could make and enforce its own statutes."[24] It embodied the purpose of gathering, holding, sharing, and disseminating knowledge. And, it saw itself as performing these functions not narrowly, but broadly.

Monastic opposition to the university appeared shortly afterward to become a characteristic of the medieval world. In the university, "the monasteries did irrevocably lose their dominance over education and scholarship to the cathedral schools."[25] But it would not be a contest between the religious and the secular as might be characterized today by monastic and university education. Instead, the "fact that monks and scholars were competing for many of the same positions in the Church partly explains the monastic opposition to the scholars,"[26] with the other part being that an even larger issue was at stake. "The expansion of the schools and the advances of scholars posed a considerable challenge to the religious and intellectual order that the monasteries and monks had dominated for so long."[27] The issue was not scientific or philosophical order over Christian theology, but which location of power, monastery or cathedral, would provide the organizing order to the

Locating the academic study of religion 31

knowledge the era produced. In other words, would the monastery retain its exclusive hold on the role of education in leading the religious life, or would there be a contender? The cathedral university became that immediate contender as well as the predecessor of the modern university.

The Church set the rules of the medieval European university, interpreted and enforced laws pertaining to students, faculty, and administration, and meted out punishments along with where and how they would be served. It was the oldest ancestor of the modern university administration. "But, if perchance such a crime has been committed that imprisonment [of a student] is necessary, the bishop shall detain the criminal in his prison . . . [and] the chancellor is forbidden to keep him in his prison."[28] The chancellor was a theological enforcer and when necessary, a jailor.

As there were no libraries and few books in the medieval world, formal classroom lectures on classic texts were the university's mechanisms of knowledge production and distribution. This would be followed by a unique paean to the organizing principles governing the university and the world it represented through its knowledge, in the exercise of "an ancient custom in this city that when a book is finished mass should be sung to the Holy Ghost."[29]

In the classrooms the Church determined what subjects were to be taught, and not taught,[30] and how. "These are the articles," begins the *Condemnation of Errors at Paris in 1241*, "rejected as contrary to true theology and condemned by Odo, the chancellor of Paris, and the masters ruling in theology at Paris . . ."[31] What we would call today disciplines of natural science and social sciences included phenomena

> concerning first matter, form, composition, generation, corruptions, each of the senses, their objects, each faculty of the soul, their operations and natures, concerning the element of nature and their operations, concerning the heavenly bodies, their natures, influences and movements . . . [with the Church's theology structuring] their orderly arrangement [so as to] be more easily understood.[32]

In *An Invective Against the New Learning*, in the late 12th century Stephen of Tournai appealed to the Pope to bring order to the scholarly pursuit of knowledge by fashioning proper boundaries for the human desire to know. The freedom to gather knowledge, which characterizes the educated life, is distinguished from intellectual license by principles of organization. Intellectual freedom was provided, protected, and given a trajectory by the Church. In his teaching, Abelard's (1079–1142) concern involved the principles organizing the "universals" which held together the "diversity" of phenomena in the world. These universals, which individuals could hardly

32 *Locating the academic study of religion*

hold the capacity to "venture to define it," found the fullest satisfaction of unity in the monastic life, the "religious" life.[33]

But as contender, the university was changing the location of where Christian theology was wielding its influence on education and how the religious life was to be lived, and Augustine stood here too as an important an influence as any. The *Charrtularium universitatis Parieiensis*, I, pp. 644–649, composed in 1286 gave a list of what the era's "university bookstore" included and under the classification of "Exemplars in Theology," Augustine numbers over 30 pieces including theological treatises, doctrinal positions, and expositions regarding the order of daily life. He was "the greatest thinker of the early Middle Ages, and his writings, at all times in the Middle Ages and in many eras of the modern world, exercised a great influence on other leading theologians and philosophers."[34] And while his treatise *On Christian Teaching* (*De doctrina christiana*) was published in the 420s as guide on "how to teach Christianity [and] not a general handbook on education," still it became "hugely influential in medieval times."[35]

Augustine shaped the intellectual environment from which education emerged out of the monastery and into its competitor, the university. He was adamant in maintaining "a balance between the precedence of authoritative faith on one hand and the positive value of human science on the other . . . [and seeking] a conceptual synthesis of these two elements."[36] For him this balance – between "religion" as Christian theology and science – guided humanity in a trajectory that aimed knowledge towards a unity knitted together by love through Christian faith. "The old analogy between *macrocosmos* (the universe as a whole) and *microcosmos* (man)"[37] is deepened in that Christian allegory would "make just as important a contribution to the understanding of nature as an objective scholarly analysis. This double view of nature would henceforth become a characteristic part of the spiritual life of the whole middle ages."[38] And likewise, university education.

Augustine was not only concerned with what to teach from the knowledge that had been gathered, but that all knowledge that is gathered, be properly organized. Before the pinnacle of Enlightenment philosophical organization in Diderot's *encyclopedie*, it was Augustine's "hope that some diligent persons may compile lists of place-names, birds, beasts, plants, and metals in the Bible . . . [and help] to bring into existence the type of learned reference book which we now think of as an encyclopedia."[39]

But even more than that, and looking through the lens of how university knowledge is organized today:

> Another rather more telling deficiency of the system [of university education] was that it lacked any superior metascience that could put the individual subject disciplines into a larger logical and philosophical

Locating the academic study of religion   33

context, based on some kind of clear theory of knowledge as such . . . Such more general questions were usually discussed in the context of theology, therefore, on the basis of the Augustinian view on the object of knowledge as the ideas which were hidden in God but could be revealed in the eternal light with which God illumined the universe. Such a concept made it impossible, among other things, to reach any clear distinction between philosophy and theology.[40]

Therefore, all philosophical debates necessarily involved theology. So did scientific ones. In "Augustine's programme . . . scientific knowledge is marginal to the scheme . . . [but not from] a fear of the natural sciences" but that ignorant theologians would "treat the book of Genesis as a source-book for science without realizing the very different purpose of the sacred book."[41] Why did Augustine fear bad theology? Bad theology yields false scientific fact. And if scientific fact "as a consequent is false, the antecedent will also be false."[42] Augustine harbored no fear of science when "faith precedes science, fixes its boundaries, and prescribes it conditions."[43]

Gradually this new way of education represented by the cathedral university changed the space and time wherein the "religious" life was learned and, as we'll see below, led. Whereas in the early medieval world the "religious" and educational life were integrated in the monastic life, by the 16th century there was a space between monastic religious life lived and university education pursued. The Reformation would be "the more dangerous world of the city and the marketplace, exposing its thinkers to pressures and problems"[44] that the ordered days of the monastery and cathedral space of the university envisioned differently.

One can see a further complexity of spatiality introduced by two new Reformation elements. The Protestant protest involved hermeneutics and the manner in which Augustine's world of the City of God and the City of Man, was transformed into a different temporal and spatial binary, one of the "two books" being interpreted: the book of scripture (the temporal world ordered by God's word) and the book of nature (the domain ordered by God's work). In the earliest era of the university both were interpreted symbolically through human active movement (Christian ritual and ceremony), but the epistemological move here was literary and empirical, and radically so. Both texts demanded differing paths to determine the true, and as multiple determinations of belief and sources of authority arose so did contestation and division. The third element, the emergence of the idea of the individual, Protestantism's "dangerous idea,"[45] can also be seen as integral to the Reformation's hermeneutical shift and its influence on education and what the study of "religion" would come to mean.

34 *Locating the academic study of religion*

This transition yielded a revolution in the university as well. One can easily see why education was critical to upholding the authority of the individual to interpret the "two books." It became the means to live the Christian life as a discerning pilgrim amidst the complexities of the worldly urban order. To be equipped and able "to read" both correctly was essential. But, fracture brought competing beliefs producing contesting ways to organize the knowledge produced by different ways of reading both books.

By the time of the Enlightenment, philosophy had firmly established itself in this breach as reasoned reflection that had dethroned Christian theology's unitary role in the university. Philosophy shaped the organizing principles of the university in a particular way, by maintaining that unlike the theology of Christendom, "philosophy had no specific content"[46] and no higher authority than human reason. It could therefore be the foundation for a more expansive view that unlike its Christian predecessor, favored no particular view. Putting forward its reflective practices as grounded in free inquiry made it ideal for selecting the truths that would unite all the strands of particularized knowledge into a cohesive, tightly stitched garment. Its single-minded allegiance to reason generated knowledge that theology simply could not with its ambiguous allegiances intertwining knowledge with Christian belief and formulation; as though philosophy and the philosophers who practiced it were absent of allegiances intellectual and otherwise.[47]

This "privileging of philosophy as a contentless and unconstrained activity, allowed Kant to retain the ideal of unified knowledge within the reality of ever more specialized university faculties."[48] In the university location this newly reigning organizing principle, philosophy altered the other two. Yet, unlike either religion or science, it promoted no particular metaphysic except that which reason could discern which, as can be seen in any intellectual history of the West, gradually favored empirical science. "From the 1830s onwards, however, the term 'science' started to refer specifically to the natural sciences and to be distinguished clearly from philosophy in both academic and general usage."[49]

But in the intellectual history within which the modern *universitas* as an epistemological project was born and raised the shift included not only Kant's epistemological grounding in reason but Hegel's critique of Kant as well. This yielded "the paradoxical result of an *ambiguous radicalization of the critique of knowledge* [which] is not an enlightened position of philosophy with regard to science. When philosophy asserts itself as authentic science, the relation of philosophy and science completely disappears from discussion."[50] In the university location the disappearance of a relationship portends the disappearance of philosophy as an epistemological organizing check and balance on science.

Locating the academic study of religion   35

When the allegiances given to philosophy were analyzed, as Marx later did, the stage was set for another shift in the unitary function of knowledge within the university context. Because "*Marx conceives of reflection according to the model of production*"[51] a context for Western intellectualism was gradually created, Positivism, which camouflaged and confirmed "the [forgetting of the] experience of reflection."[52] And without philosophical reflection differentiated from science, there is no mechanism in the university for the consideration of allegiances. Thus, in terms of the university's unitary organizing principles the shift from theology to philosophy was heralded as a triumph of reflection rooted in reason over allegiance rooted in formulation; only to yield, in a subsequent shift from philosophy to science, a return to allegiance rooted in formulation.

But Enlightenment philosophy also altered the understanding of what constituted religion. Now it's possible to see how in the former era "religion" was synonymous with Christian theology, whereas Enlightenment philosophy's organizing of knowledge "signaled the beginning of the process of transposing 'religion' from a supernatural to a natural history, from a theological to an anthropological category."[53] "Religion" changed from the unified conception as medieval Christendom into the binary of Christian theology and natural religion.

In its ascent to prominence as the university's organizing principle, philosophy had split one rival into theology, governed by a particular allegiance, and natural religion as a philosophically suitable universal concept, and laid the foundation in reason for the eventual ascent of its other rival, science. As the university's epistemological organizing principles changed once again, ushering in the modern age, the university worked to craft knowledge gathered by disciplines and tied into a unitary whole by science. This organization form was confirmed as the foundation of knowledge in the modern American state's move to privilege university research as joining scientific progress to civic virtue in the 1944 report, *Science: The Endless Frontier*:

> Laying out a plan for the future of university-based research, [Dr. Vannevar] Bush observed that "[s]cientific progress is one essential key to our security as a nation, to our better health, to more jobs, to a higher standard of living, and to our cultural progress." To achieve these outcomes, he proposed a system in which government funding would flow into universities for four key purposes: to create new knowledge, educate the next generation of scientists, create new products and industries, and advance the public welfare.[54]

36 *Locating the academic study of religion*

In the ascent of science over philosophy and the now twofold understanding of religion as Christian theology and the universal natural religion, there were consequences for epistemology and academic study of any kind:

> Positivism marks the end of the theory of knowledge. In its place emerges the philosophy of science . . . Knowledge is implicitly defined by the achievement of the sciences.[55]

Over the past two centuries philosophy and religion both have become servants of a newly ordained source of epistemological principles for organizing and ordering:

> For the philosophy of science that has emerged since the mid-nineteenth century as the heir of the theory of knowledge is methodology pursued with a scientistic self-understanding of the sciences. "Scientism" means science's belief in itself; that is, the conviction that we can no longer understand science as one form of possible knowledge, but rather must identify knowledge with science.[56]

And although science is "increasingly seen not as a neutral account of phenomena based on the pursuit of pure knowledge, but as a way of making sense of the world, one influenced by the contexts within which scientific problems are framed, discussed, and 'solved,'"[57] it remains the driving unitary epistemological force in the university, segmented as it is into disciplines and as a pervasive influence and allegiance through "the principle of scientism . . . [which] is that the meaning of knowledge is defined by what the sciences do and can thus be adequately explicated through the methodological analysis of scientific procedures."[58]

It is within this epistemological context and culture that discourses and lines of inquiry still develop and are deemed by academics to be of interest or not, including the study of religion. Allegiances form in disciplinary departments, personnel committee decision-making, collegial organizations, academic conferences, and all the various expanses of professionalism. They're shaped by lawmakers and which economic forecasters are holding sway at any given time. Allegiances also form as lines of intellectual inquiry are deemed as interesting, and these allegiances can be traced back along the lines of inquiry to rest in disciplinary concepts and methodologies, shaped as they are by the university's unitary organizing principles.

In its ascent to prominence as the university's organizing and ordering principle, science had subdued one rival, philosophy, taken the split in its other and relegated theology to a supernatural metaphysical contender/pretender, and entrenched the assumption of religion as a universal reality.

Locating the academic study of religion 37

This laid the foundation for the religious studies predicament of occupying two competing domains. First, the domain of the university where science is still the epistemological organizing principle and, thus, questions arise by other faculty and administration like those in my university location when considering the creation of a religious studies program. And, the domain of the field itself where the concept of religion has been and continues to be historicized and rejected as universal, the pursuit of a full science of religions has been laid to rest and grieved, and uncertainties abound ranging from "Why Still 'Religion'?"[59] to "what is so bad about foundering around?"[60] In an ironic twist and a nod to Whitehead's estimation, in both form and principle within the modern university location, science precedes religion, fixes its boundaries, and prescribes its conditions!

A cluster of additional characteristics of interdisciplinary study

It could be that a robust religious studies is now not possible and its foundering around even to the point of what it should call itself is evidence of demise. But it could also be that its current condition is a harbinger of the limitations of the epistemological product the modern university produces through its current structures and organizing principles. When problems outside the university require a broader academic response than what current university structures and epistemological organization can deliver as, for example, in the issue of what to do with wetlands, academics from environmental studies, biology, political science, business, and public policy are often consulted for an integrative solution. The product has to be interdisciplinary produced or it is not of pragmatic value. Why would that not be the case in some activities outside the university that involve phenomena as broad and complex as religious ones, and demand an understanding of some sort even when inside academia scholars struggle with whether the concept of "religion" is a comprehensive and useful one? It's not that interior conversations circumscribing the field and its concepts aren't productive, but they are in certain ways specific to a locational domain. Compiling a cluster of interdisciplinarity's characteristics helps identify in what situations this style of performing hermeneutics might be of use.

The historical portion of this chapter represents a foundational characteristic of interdisciplinarity as well as what the religious studies scholar needs. It is rooted in a critique of the university as an epistemological project structured through disciplinarity. In addition to this attention to professional location, the interdisciplinary scholar is grounded also in a self-consciousness concerning personal location akin to that in autoethnographic and indigenous methodologies, and integrates the two locations as part of the process

38   *Locating the academic study of religion*

of generating a new space for knowledge to be constructed. Painstakingly, the interdisciplinary religious studies scholar searches the history of how academia has studied what it has studied, including "religion" and how the conceptual understanding of what it was changed in various historical and cultural locations; and with a special emphasis on how since the middle 19th century that study fulfilled and pushed against scientific organizing principles in the modern academic milieu. The scholar aligns with those who study disciplinary methodologies to employ their rigor to push beyond disciplinarity's rigidity without becoming captive to eclecticism. The interdisciplinary religious studies scholar can articulate the distinctions between university structure and organization today and in the past, and how relevant disciplinary domains are distinct and overlapping, including theology, philosophy, the social sciences, and political science and cultural studies. Finally, a distinction can be made between participating in the university location and engaging the phenomenon whose activity is to be studied outside the university location, especially in the overlap and shifting boundaries of insider/outside domains.

As a dialogic style of research, interdisciplinarity is in conversation with two locations, the university from which the scholar comes and will return, and the world outside where phenomena are engaged and studied. Collaboration is necessary in both locations. In engaging phenomena requiring scientific and public policy determinations, such as the wetlands example above, an interdisciplinary style involves teams of experts who bring their disciplinary scholarship into a unified analysis and prescription. A knowledge and self-conscious use of interdisciplinarity is critical in those cases. In contrast religious studies scholars appear more solitary in their epistemological pursuits so the collaboration practiced must be a "double self-conscious" one, self-reflexive in intention and multiple in effect. The religious studies scholar is in collaborative dialogue with communities of scholars not just in the academic study of religion but also in the disciplines the scholar is actively using and being guided towards, including with interdisciplinarity itself. The interdisciplinary scholar also constructs and maintains a different kind of collaborative relationship with the active insiders observed in the location outside the university, one that while informed by protocols and best practices designed in the university is fashioned on the site of study.

While interdisciplinarity begins with a critique of disciplinarity as an epistemological structure, it is not a repudiation of it. "Only within a world of disciplines can one be interdisciplinary."[61] Collaboration here means that disciplinary knowledge production is part of the process of starting in the university, going out to engage phenomena, and returning to the university location to construct new knowledge. Disciplinarity models the stability methodologies must possess to maintain rigor and offers knowledge born of

Locating the academic study of religion 39

that rigor as scientifically designed and measured within the university. But, while rigor may be steadfast it also incompletely accounts for phenomena in their context outside the university where they occur. A concept conceived in the university is not as broad and complex as phenomena engaged outside the university, and the aim of interdisciplinarity in creating a new space upon the scholar's return is to account for what disciplinary methodology and results cannot. In this way interdisciplinary collaboration aims towards a flexibility the disciplines cannot long sustain. In-between the disciplines does not mean ignoring disciplinary yield but using it with a different aim. Thus, the "disciplines are not the focus of the interdisciplinarian's attention"[62] in that the pursuit in collaboration involves "overcome[ing] some of the fragmentation of knowledge"[63] harbored in the current university location. Yet, the disciplines employed by the scholar must "recognize themselves" and their lines of inquiry in the product the interdisciplinary scholar generates.

The collaboration that characterizes using an interdisciplinary style with methodologies in religious studies is not confined or even primarily delineated by working with other religious studies scholars. It doesn't mean there is no consultation with colleagues in religious studies, but that "interdisciplinary" means interaction amongst disciplines and generating knowledge that is the end result of a scholar's deliberate process of integrating disciplinary products. The scholar who primarily or exclusively works with religious studies scholars at their university and at professional meetings does not perform interdisciplinarity because the process of collaboration is different.

This complex and layered understanding of location becomes necessary and useful as the scholar engages phenomena outside the university. The knowledge that the interdisciplinary scholar will generate is not in opposition or disregard towards any location inside the university or out, but through understanding the intersection of locations as constituting a positionality that accounts for them as pivotal to collaborative work.

As many lay claim to employing interdisciplinarity, it becomes an admittedly slippery thing to grasp if one tries to hold it by definition, an approach favored in disciplinarity. One way to identify it is to distinguish it from other "extra-disciplinary" forms of epistemological assembling: "*Multidisciplinarity* [has been] defined as an approach that juxtaposes disciplines . . . foster[ing] wider knowledge, information, and methods."[64] Whereas a disciplinary approach to the study of religion involves asking a psychologist or sociologist to define religion, trying to squeeze all phenomena into what can be captured through one lens of information gathering and ordering, a multidisciplinary approach to the same study entails gathering the psychologist and sociologist into the same room with a philosopher and anthropologist

40   *Locating the academic study of religion*

and theologian to discuss a definition of religion. Distinct, disciplinary conversations would occur alongside of one another. Yet, while disciplinary pursuits yield greater clarity in detail, a product of specialization, and multidisciplinary ones yield a wider breadth to gathered knowledge, the result might be invigorating but through "experiencing little [necessary] contact between the participating disciplines."[65] Yet, when "integration and interaction become proactive, the line between multidisciplinarity and interdisciplinarity is crossed."[66] While multidisciplinarity can be "defined as an approach that juxtaposes disciplines . . . integration of disciplines [is] the 'litmus test' of interdisciplinarity."[67]

The scholar's work in the university both before and after engaging the phenomenon "out there" must involve integration because interdisciplinarity itself is "a process of answering a question, solving a problem, or addressing a topic that is too broad or complex to be dealt with adequately by a single discipline or profession."[68] The epistemological goal is the creative synthesis of the disciplinary products that initially went into the formulation of concepts as performed from the academic location of religious studies in the university; with the dynamic activity of insiders performing as practitioners residing within a domain of overlapping orders seen and shared with the scholar, and unseen and shared with other insiders; with the activity of the scholar returning to the university location not to confirm originating concepts and theories but to have them transformed by engaging phenomena in its location. Synthesis distinguishes interdisciplinary product from the epistemological collective that is multidisciplinary. While disciplines include in their locations synthesis of various lines of inquiry and contests amongst theoreticians, there is a boundary however indefinite it may appear that, when transgressed, elicits cries of sloppiness in disciplinary rigor or the creation of a new discipline. Disciplinary integration involves a rigor evaluated by some level of adherence to the concepts of the discipline and is measurable by how skillfully they are employed using the acknowledged methods of the discipline. Thus, synthesis in the disciplinary context always presses against the question of the boundary of the discipline and from the standpoint of interdisciplinarity, too many times succumbs to the reductionism it is always flirting with.

As is the case in other aspects of its style, the synthesis that characterizes interdisciplinary integration on the other hand starts from a positionality critiquing the disciplines. It does not pose whether the knowledge-producing process fulfills disciplinary boundaries, but how skillfully the interdisciplinarian has manipulated disciplinary yields to create concepts that are useful in a phenomenal location housing activity outside the university. Interdisciplinary integration involves a rigor evaluated by comprehensiveness; that is, by depth, breadth, and range in the synthesis between the disciplinary

Locating the academic study of religion 41

yields initially consulted in the generation of the concepts in the university location, the vigor of the scholar's engagement with the activity when studied in its location, and the reconsideration of concept that is part of the methodology of knowledge production back in the university setting. Questions are not predominantly of the kind measuring how true the scholar was to concepts and methodologies, tools and blueprints devised within the scholar's study and with other like-minded scholars, but how flexible and yet still comprehensible concepts are in the scholar's use coming back into the study after engaging activity outside. Synthesis involves how useful the yield is to disciplines the scholar drew upon, how coherent the yield is to other religious studies scholars doing similar work, and how the result generated a newly created space for knowledge to be constructed. In other words, as the product of integration the synthesis that is interdisciplinary involves exercising stable methodology using concepts containing dynamic elasticity that provide coherent understanding of activity outside the university and inside its own distinct location.

The rise of religious studies in the context of the university as an epistemological project

From the latter decades of the 20th century and into the 21st interdisciplinarity has emerged as an approach to analyzing and evaluating the context of academia as an epistemological project, and has become a trajectory for the production of new knowledge and the construction of new interpretations by breaking through disciplinary constraints formed by that project. In the book *Interdisciplinarity*, Joe Moran traced its rise as an inherently transformative approach to the gathering and ordering of knowledge: "In this sense, interdisciplinarity interlocks with the concerns of epistemology . . . and tends to be centred around problems and issues that cannot be addressed or solved within the existing disciplines, rather than the quest for an all-inclusive synthesis."[69] Within the modern university, interdisciplinarity had its origins in the English Department since

> it is possible to argue that all the major critical developments and controversies within English since its inception as a university subject have been related in some sense to the difficulty of containing its concerns with a single discipline and to its interdisciplinary possibilities.[70]

It could be said of the phenomenon that formed the object of its study "that literature is about everything . . . and this is hard to accommodate within the narrow parameters of a discipline."[71] Similar qualities could be put forward regarding religious studies. It involves human activity that is various and

42 *Locating the academic study of religion*

about everything, and in terms of the university is part of its historic epistemological organizing principles alongside of philosophy and in competition with science. As interdisciplinarity involves "some kind of critical awareness of this relationship [between knowledge and power],"[72] this becomes central to understanding religious studies as it came to be developed.

The move from philosophy to science as the university's organizing principle is also the context within which the academic study of religion came about on the heels of the Enlightenment's transforming religion as Christian theology into religion as Christian theology and natural religion. Like interdisciplinarity's appearance, the modern study of religion began with questions generated from the encounter with texts and language, as the breadth of European colonialism in the 19th century accelerated the encounter of Christianity with a whole diversity of texts from religious traditions that bore foreign languages, theologies, and metaphysics. At first scholars engaged the study of non-Christian texts as the chief means to understand beliefs. But, gradually this textual bias yielded to more of what we now see as social scientific analysis. Thus, interdisciplinarity and the modern form of the academic study of religion were each rooted in the 19th century's linguistic turn and share the location's intellectual trajectory. Gradually the study of the spiritual expressions of "others" was taken up by the emerging social sciences as they were launched and developed within the university. Declarations were made by anthropologists, sociologists, and psychologists as to what "natural religion" was, what it involved, how it functioned, and where it could be seen. Allegiances to these disciplinary silos were formed and deepened, still influenced by Christian theological categories left over from the university's earliest days when "religion" meant Christendom. It is not necessary here to delineate the details of that development so expertly detailed elsewhere by others, except to highlight its 20th-century trajectory and its 21st-century repositioning seen through the lens of interdisciplinary critique.

The 20th century's chief pursuit was to create the History of Religions, the scientific study of religion, and Mircea Eliade along with others gave justification to that endeavor within the university's organizing and ordering principle, science. It was the century's great undertaking. The History of Religions would circumscribe the sacred as a universal object of study. New concepts and methods would be developed alongside of older ones, with the effect, intentional or not, of a line of inquiry becoming an academic discipline in the scientifically structured university:

> a religious phenomenon will only be recognized as such if it is grasped at its own level, that is to say, if it is studied *as* something religious. To try to grasp the essence of such phenomenon by means of physiology,

Locating the academic study of religion 43

psychology, sociology, economics, linguistics, art or any other study is false; it misses the one unique and irreducible element in it – the element of the sacred.[73]

In this declaration Eliade outlined what he thought was being missed by other disciplines in order to argue for the inclusion of the "science of religions" in the university's disciplinary pantheon. He maintained Durkheim's binary distinction between the sacred and profane, and installed it the foundation stone of this new scientific endeavor. His new articulation of the university's long-standing, binary view of this human activity, the two-world-domain hypothesis, no longer the twin cities of Augustinian Christian theology nor the "division of the world into two domains . . . [wherein] the fact of the contrast is universal"[74] harbored dimensions of *homo religiosus* camouflaged by contemporary disciplines. Located in the domain of the profane, the university had a means to study scientifically human religious activity in the domain of the sacred.

The argument over whether and what was being missed by other disciplines continued into the 21th century. As part of the developing discourse a refutation of Eliade's claim coalesced vis-à-vis historicizing critiques from postmodernism, post-colonialism, et al. Social constructionist arguments over the historical and cultural origins of "religion," its uses for colonialist subjugation and domination, and the political biases of religious theories and of religious theorists like Eliade and others constructed something new. The concept of "religion" underwent another transformation. In the medieval European origins of the university as representing "the ideal of making the teaching body representative of the whole cycle of human knowledge"[75] organized by "religion" as Christian theology involving the City of God and the City of Man, to the Enlightenment philosophical transformation of "religion" into Christian theology and "natural religion," was added another metamorphosis summarized thus: "by eliminating Mircea Eliade's conjunction 'and' in his well-known title, *The Sacred and the Profane: The Nature of Religion*, we intend to dispel the notion that these two designators name separate domains that somehow interact from time to time."[76] The two-world hypothesis could be conflated to one, a reduction of domains suitable to the modern university as disciplinarily structured and organized by scientific principles.

Eliade's attempt to delimit a component of a phenomena camouflaged by the disciplinary structures of the university, in order to justify a new venture supported by the organizing epistemological principles of the university, was deflated by historicizing critiques. These critiques still operate in the university as an attempted corrective to all disciplines and fields in the university by relativizing for the concepts and methods for each. Interdisciplinarity

44 *Locating the academic study of religion*

contributed to this critique by relativizing the epistemological product of the university itself, including these very critiques as generated by disciplinary structure and unified by the principles of science; that is, the characteristics of this particular location at this time. But for religious studies, born in the dreams of science and disciplines, the critique bore the future of an illusion:

> Our first assumption is that the modern western research university is a purpose-designed institution for obtaining knowledge about the world . . . [and] is successful only when it is not in service of ideological, theological, and religious agendas. Rather, its primary objective is scientific, that is, to gain public (intersubjectively available) knowledge of public (intersubjectively available) facts . . . We now understand that we were both deluded by our overly optimistic but cognitively naïve expectations of the development of a truly scientific field for the study of religion in the context of a modern, research university.[77]

The promise of a scientific study of religion suitable to the modern university's epistemological requirements has decentralized the field into multiple centers with little clarity as to how the centers are or could be organized in an epistemic relationship. New lines of inquiry are being produced with invigorating research and new prospects for knowledge production in evidence. Yet, there is a pervasive uncertainty as to how all of this holds together in a common field in the modern university. Interdisciplinarity does not hold the promise of that organizing principle as it is only a style of performing methodology. But, its critique identifies another version of the West's ongoing two-world-domain hypothesis emerging from the university: the insiders' various domains as they reside within them and outside the scholar's study and university hallways, and the conversation about the sacred and profane as related to a changed concept of "religion" going on inside the scholar's study domain. It is from this critique that a new space, a third domain emerges by interdisciplinary retooling of foundational concepts for use in interdisciplinary endeavors.

Notes

1 N. Ross Reat, 1983, pp. 459–476.
2 David Tracy, 1994, p. 16.
3 Julie Thompson Klein, 2010, p. 17.
4 Steve Fuller, 2010, p. 51.
5 Preamble, "Association for Interdisciplinary Studies." Retrieved at: https://oakland.edu/ais/about/mission/
6 See Joe Moran, *Interdisciplinarity*, Routledge, Abingdon, UK, 2002. Print.
7 See *Oxford Handbook of Interdisciplinarity*, Robert Frodeman, editor, Oxford, 2010. Print.

Locating the academic study of religion 45

8 Moran, 2002, p. 15.
9 Marilyn Preston, 2018, p. 1.
10 H. Chang, 2008, pp. 48–49 as quoted by Boylorn and Orbe, editors, 2014, p. 17.
11 Moran, 2002, p. 5.
12 Alfred North Whitehead, 1929, p. 11.
13 Alfred North Whitehead, 1938, p. 67.
14 Ibid., p. 44.
15 Moran, 2002, p. 4.
16 Alfred North Whitehead, 1926, p. 57.
17 Ibid.
18 Moran, 2002, p. 8.
19 Ibid., p. 10.
20 "Statutes of Robert De Courcon for Paris in 1215," quoted in *The Medieval World: 300–1300*, p. 305.
21 Stephen C. Ferruolo, 1985. Print, p. 5.
22 Ibid., p. 2.
23 Alister McGrath, 2007, p. 326.
24 Ibid., p. 4.
25 Ibid., p. 50.
26 Ibid., p. 48.
27 Ibid.
28 "Statutes of Gregory IX for the University of Paris in 1231," quoted in *The Medieval World: 300–1300*, p. 303.
29 Charles Homer Haskins, 1923, p. 61.
30 "Statutes of Robert De Courcon for Paris in 1215," 1968, p. 305.
31 "Condemnation of Errors at Paris in 1241," quoted in *The Medieval World: 300–1300*, pp. 306–307.
32 Lynn Thorndike, 1944, p. 144.
33 Ibid., pp. 4–5.
34 Norman F. Cantor, "The Augustinian World-View," *The Medieval World: 300–1300*, 1968, p. 37.
35 Henry Chadwick, 2009, p. 82.
36 Olaf Pedersen, 1997, p. 63.
37 Ibid., p. 65.
38 Ibid.
39 Chadwick, 2009, p. 84.
40 Pedersen, 1997, p. 276.
41 Chadwick, 2009, p. 86.
42 Ibid., p. 83.
43 Haskins, 1923, p. 71, quoting Alzog, *Church History* (1876), II, p. 733.
44 McGrath, 2007, p. 319.
45 Ibid., p. 2.
46 Moran, 2002, p. 9.
47 Ryan Gillespie, 2014, p. 4.
48 Moran, 2002, pp. 9–10.
49 Ibid.
50 Jurgen Habermas, 1971, p. 24.
51 Ibid., p. 44.
52 Ibid., p. vii.
53 Smith, 1998, p. 273.
54 Joseph E. Aoun, 1945. Retrieved at: https://nsf.gov/about/history/vbush1945.htm

46 *Locating the academic study of religion*

55 Habermas, 1971, p. 67.
56 Ibid., p. 4.
57 Moran, 2002, p. 155.
58 Habermas, 1971, p. 67.
59 Hent de Vries, 2008.
60 Robert Orsi, 2016, p. 264.
61 Stephen Toulmin, 2001, p. 140.
62 A. F. Repko, 2012, p. 5.
63 R. C. Miller, 1982, p. 3.
64 Julie Thompson Klein, 2010, p. 17.
65 Raymond C. Miller, 1982, p. 6.
66 Moran, 2002, p. 18.
67 Klein, 2010, p. 17.
68 Julie T. Klein and William Newell, 1997.
69 Moran, 2002, p. 15.
70 Ibid., p. 19.
71 Ibid., p. 21.
72 Ibid., p. 3.
73 Micrea Eliade, 1958, p. xvii.
74 Emile Durkheim, 1915, pp. 37, 39.
75 Stephen C. Ferruolo, 1985, p. 2.
76 William Arnal and Russell McCutcheon, 2012, p. xi.
77 Luther H. Martin and Donald Wiebe, 2014, p. 1129.

2 Something other than an "and" or an "is"

The overlapping domain of the sacred-profane

One of the responsibilities of a parish minister in the congregations I served involved being present with persons as they were dying, and their families during the dying and grieving process. In 27 years of performing that role I have been with people breathing their last breaths, in the presence of bodies that one moment were moving and the next minute not, some as anticipated following a long physical decline, some unexpected. I've been with young parents as their newly born twins' tiny bodies expired, a mother at the hospital as she identified the drowned body of her boy, a husband as his wife of ten years died in their home, and parents in shock at the murder of their child. I've been with families afterward, with people who have attempted to climb into caskets with their dead loved ones, have scattered ashes in places designated as special by individuals or families or communities, and told a mother her adolescent son had killed himself with a shotgun. It is a too-obvious observation to point out that all events involving the boundary between life and death are distinctive in their own ways while at the same time each moment contains a heightened quality generating deep human emotion. Whether the emotion is guided towards the situation or is enlisted in the linguistic cognitive response is unclear, but anecdotally the context of insiders with location involves a deep absorption that disorients and dislocates. "Are your affairs in order?"

Has it always been that way in history? I do not know. Is it that way in all cultures? Again, I cannot say. Human activity can be and has been studied by anthropology, sociology, psychology, philosophy, neurology, even political science and cultural studies in terms of this boundary, and now in affect theory. Different university disciplinary approaches view different aspects of the two domains, life and death, and use different measurements in theorizing. Theologies are produced relative to each domain.

For a religious studies scholar to study interdisciplinarily the function of human activity regarding these two domains, there is a process. First, to trace the history of the conceptual organization of the two domains within

48   *Something other than an "and" or an "is"*

the context of the larger history of the university as an epistemological project. Second, to take that preparation inside the university outside to moments and activities in the context that is *not* the university to see how university epistemological concepts are transformed through that encounter. And third, bring that encounter back into the university location in order to generate a new space in-between the disciplines in which new knowledge and understanding can appear.

The choice of an activity outside the university as extreme as those involving life and death is purposeful. It's suited to an interdisciplinary style of performing methodology in religious studies, as there is a history and tradition of conceiving of study in this way:

> it always leads to a better understanding of a thing's significance to consider its exaggerations and perversions, its equivalents and substitutes and nearest relatives elsewhere . . . [for] phenomena are best understood when placed within their series, studied in their germ and in their over-ripe decay, and compared with their exaggerated and degenerated kindred.[1]

Given the limitations of our study here it can still be said that considering the boundary of the two conceptual-and-related domains in the development of the university as an epistemological project – the sacred and the secular, and the sacred and the profane – this binary conceptual design brought out of the university in order to engage a phenomenon (the exaggerated and over-ripe moment of moving from life to death) can tell us much about conceptual usefulness in understanding the function of human activity responding affectively – that is, bodily and cognitively – to those moments. How has this binary conceptual design been fitted to the development of the epistemological purposes of the university location? Is there a space in-between generated by taking those concepts into direct engagement with phenomena as we are considering it here? Does the human being as an embodied entity residing in time and place respond to moments exaggerating the boundary between life and death, with activity that functions in-between the concepts of the sacred and secular, and sacred and profane as developed in the university as a historically and culturally constructed location?

Yet, in interdisciplinarity, work on concepts and methods as historical/cultural products of the university as an epistemological project, is but the first step. "To understand a thing rightly we need to see it both out of its environment and in it, and to have acquaintance with the whole range of its variations."[2] Eventually, to satisfy the designation of interdisciplinary, we need to move beyond the scholar's study as the location and the scholar's self-consciousness as the object of study, to engage the first order experience of this moment *in extremis*. Then, return to reconsider the space in-between.

The changing reputation of a binary conceptual design

It is within the epistemological context and culture of the modern university that discourses and lines of inquiry still develop and are deemed by academics to be of interest or not, including the study of religion. Allegiances are formed in disciplinary departments, personnel committee decision-making, collegial organizations, academic conferences, and all the various expanses of professionalism. They're shaped by lawmakers and the economic forecasting that is holding sway at any given time. Allegiances also form as lines of intellectual inquiry are deemed as interesting, and these allegiances can be traced back along the lines of inquiry to rest in disciplinary concepts and methodologies, shaped as they are by the university's unitary organizing principles which today come from science.

When I returned to academia 27 years after my graduate school days and needing to prepare myself for residence in my new professional location. I discovered the field had moved, and is still moving through a reconsideration of its identity in the modern university, and of the concepts that since the advent of science as constituting the organizing principles of university produced knowledge, formed the core of studying this dimension of human activity: the sacred and profane. There were portions of the field eyeing the scholar's study as the proper object of study, others that announced and grieved the loss of a science of religions, and still others venturing outside the university to continue encountering human religious activity. There developed a general awareness of the historical and cultural roots of the concept of "religion," and development of the encounter between people toting that concept into cultures and histories where it wasn't. I knew from my experience that outside the university there were all kinds of current activities occurring beyond the scholar's study that could benefit from understandings the field of religious studies could offer. How did the viewpoint develop within the university, as it itself had been constructed over millennia, such that this aspect of human activity was being in the way it was?

How was the university's epistemological positionality constructed? And, what is the history of the university context wherein a conceptual framework arose constructing a "sacred" that was juxtaposed against another, the "secular," first referring to twin ontological realms of human activity; later to be transformed into distinct regions of competing allegiance; and finally in the scientific disciplines of the social and natural sciences, and then political science as distinct and rival domains, modifying the "secular" into the "profane" in the social scientific location first to denote the pair as opposites, the sacred and the (now) profane, to which was added the camouflaged conflation of one into the other, the sacred is the profane? While the original designation of the sacred and the secular becomes in our own

50 *Something other than an "and" or an "is"*

day the religious and secular – prominent still in the hard sciences to denote the scientific/theology contest and in political science in the secularization theory and its prognosis as a useful conceptual construct – our main interest here will be what becomes the sacred and profane. Since the university is an epistemological project, tracing this development will partly outline what the field looks at and how; that is, its positionality. Since the interdisciplinary process begins internally in the university, this is our starting point.

The West has a long history of imagining the study of human beings, being religious, and understanding how that is epistemologically conceptualized is relative to a given era. Yet its roots involve what could be called a two-world domain hypothesis. In the West studying human religious activity within the university involves circumscribing and accounting for the observed, binary relationship between human activity in the material world and its effect in a domain of something more. The conceptual strategies and history of constructing the two-world domains and their relationship involve the university's organizing principles in particular eras. That's what guides conceptual construction that is put forward as the accepted positionality for knowledge construction. As chronicled in the previous chapter the origin of the university in 12th century European medieval Christendom gave this study its binary foundation and a trajectory regarding knowledge gathering, ordering, and disseminating still operational today. It constitutes the university's positionality origin story.

At the time of the medieval founding of the first universities the concept of "religion" had a cultic meaning referring to ritual ceremony, and the "only distinctively Christian usage was the fifth-century extension of this cultic sense to the totality of an individuals' life in monasticism: 'religion,' a life found by monastic vows; 'religious,' a monk; 'to enter religion,' to join a monastery."[3] And as previously noted, the *universitas* developed alongside the monastery and then surpassed the monastery as the locus of education. The concept of the secular, associated in our time with science and in secularization theory found to be the opposite of religion, was derived from the Latin, *secularis*, as pertaining to time. It denoted the temporal, a long period of time likened unto to an era or epoch within which one was living. In terms of the concept of time "religion" concerned its finality. It denoted a spatial order or residence in relationship to monastic space where residence shaped how the "religious life" was lived and understood:

> In [the low Middle Ages] *saecularizatio* referred to a monk's renunciation of the rule of his order, his exit from the monastery, his return to the world, and more specifically to his transfer to the worldly or secular clergy that ministered to the laity. Importantly, a secularized priest retained traces of his monastic past: he was required to wear the

Something other than an "and" or an "is" 51

emblem of his order. This layer adds both a spatial and an individual dimension to the concept, spatial, insofar as the sacred space of the monastery is opposed to the profane space of the world; and individual, insofar as the departure of the monk implies a loss of heart or commitment, if not of belief itself.[4]

As has been noted, medieval Christendom's theological framework gave the university its initial epistemological organizing principles, and while Christian historical theologians have analyzed the Christian composition of the time, Augustine's influence remains as important as any. The conceptual development of the two world domain as part of the university's epistemological organization bore an Augustinian likeness. Augustine regarded the City of God and the City of Man as comprising spatial domains, "their mutually exclusive character, which Augustine always emphasizes when defining them formally."[5] As concepts these bore an urban metaphor of location and juxtaposition, a binary of ordered domains whereby "each [was] contained within its own sociological milieu."[6] While sociologically distinct, the sacred order of place and time, the City of God, and the secular order of place and time, the City of Man, nevertheless overlapped in the temporal conditions of existence. The function of human activity was within a temporally experienced location that simultaneously intertwined and integrated elements of its doppelganger domain so as to confer a distinctive quality.[7] Though idealized as opposites they overlapped in human existence and activity.

Thus, the concept of "religion" was composed of the concepts of time and space/place as "components inseparable *within itself*,"[8] that is, within the concept of "religion," and it was this inseparable quality that composed the concept and its relational opposition. The City of God designated a time or space/place bearing a conceptual quality in addition to whatever qualities composed the *saeculum*. But, it was integrated and intertwined with the secular. The two spatial orders were categorized sociologically as opposites but under the temporal conditions of existence they were indistinct. Human beings experienced them as overlapping domains under the umbrella of Christendom and delineated by Christian theology.

> Augustine's theology rejected the dichotomy of sacred and profane displayed in this image [of two distinct cities]. Sacred and profane, for him, interpenetrate in the *saeculum*; the "secular" is neutral, ambivalent, but no more profane than it is sacred . . . there is a real distinction to be drawn between them, but it is eschatological rather than sociological or historical. They are separable only in the final judgment, and their distinct – but not separate – being here and now in the *saeculum*

52 *Something other than an "and" or an "is"*

> consists of the relation they bear to that judgment. So in the last resort the Church *is* the world, the world reconciled in Christ.[9]

Education existed in the overlapping spatial order of both God and man in monastic life as the unitary and integrated "religious life," and then gradually, as it moved into the university and a cathedral location, education ventured out of its integrative monastic location within the "religious life" and into an additional location and space that was, not inconsequentially, set apart. While monastic life continued the integration of education and the "religious life," there now was a competitor, a domain not as immersive in its integration of the two cities into one life. The university still organized itself epistemologically through the two-world domain shaped by Augustine's Christian conceptual design, and science and philosophy still served the Queen of the Sciences through this design. But having flowed outside the integrative monastic location and into an urban location, while metaphorically consistent with Augustine's two-world domain positionality, helped change the positionality of the university as an epistemological project in the changes brought about in the Reformation and the subsequent Enlightenment.

Moving into the rupture the Reformation would become, the university held close an Augustinian conception of "religion," comprehensively Christian in character and scope, to be defended theologically.[10] The City of God/City of Man was an imaginative construct of Christianity's perspective on the interplay between two spatial and temporal domains involving human residence. One was existential, the other transcendental, but integrated, a continuous, whole-body sensation within which the scholar also resided. It was not residence in the sense of an insider location of participant relative to an outside location of scholarly observer, but residence as an undifferentiated, singular location in time and space. Philosophy may have been a handmaiden of truth but theology was the queen, as the scholastics evidenced in using the former in service to the latter. And in terms of science, it was understood that Christian doctrines buttressed a unitary meaning and purpose to the knowledge that was gathered.

The rupture of Christian unity in the Reformation yielded a doctrinal contest involving competing beliefs. It impacted the university's epistemological positionality in several important ways. First, in terms of the binary two-world domain concept, Christianity transformed the City of Man and the City of God into a different binary of structured orders of time and space, the Book of Nature and the Book of Scripture. The change from an urban to a literary metaphor favored the development of hermeneutics and philosophical methods for how to read the two books as the spatial and temporal orders within which human beings reside. At this time in the

Something other than an "and" or an "is" 53

developing epistemology of the university, when considering the Book of Nature it gradually became more and more "philosophically and empirically clear that the moving body moves not just in any sort of world, but in an earthly world, a world that is not devoid of place but laden with it."[11] A way to interpret nature as its own "book" distinct from, but related to the Book of Scripture gradually arose. Interpreting the Book of Scripture reflected the contestation of Christian beliefs fostered by the fracturing of Christian unity. *Sola scriptura* upheld and compounded the fracturing, along with a complete relocation of the religious life from the spatial and temporal order of the monastery, now only one "kind" of living the religious life, to the city, the world outside the monastery. The university prepared persons for living the "religious life" in the world not as a specialized order of time and space, but a wider, more variously unbounded order. These were conditions within which arose "the dangerous new idea, firmly embodied at the heart of the Protestant revolution . . . that all Christians have the right to interpret the Bible for themselves."[12]

This fracturing of the university's previous epistemological organizing principle had consequences ensconced in the Enlightenment. Philosophy ascended as the epistemological organizing principle that could lay a foundation for the scientific study of the Book of Nature, as well as hermeneutical endeavors appropriate to use upon the Book of Scripture. And in relationship to the spatial and temporal order – the world within which human being was immersed and the domain wherein human being developed a sense of presence – wherein the "religious life" and all other "kinds" of living took place, philosophy would provide a foundation.

> Here [in "What Is Enlightenment?"] Kant outlines a public/private distinction, making the move of identifying the reasons that matter, the best possible justifications, as those that are public-namely, free from religious, familial, revelatory natures: "The *public* use of reason must at all times be free, and it alone can bring about enlightenment among men; the *private* use of reason, however, may often be very narrowly restricted without the progress of enlightenment being particularly hindered" (1996a, 59–60, emphasis his). What is important here is both the universalizing impulse of public reason-reasons that would count for all, under all circumstances ("before the entire public of the reading world" [60]) and the connection of public reason with enlightenment, with being educated, advanced and improving.[13]

Unlike Christian theology, "philosophy had no specific content"[14] and no higher authority than human reason, and in providing the chief epistemological organizing principles for the university location modern empirical

54 *Something other than an "and" or an "is"*

science arose alongside of a radical change in the nature and organizational structure of the study of "religion."

> The fundamental idea of Kant's "critical philosophy" – especially in his three Critiques: the *Critique of Pure Reason* (1781, 1787), the *Critique of Practical Reason* (1788), and the *Critique of the Power of Judgment* (1790) – is human autonomy. He argues that the human understanding is the source of the general laws of nature that structure all our experience; and that human reason gives itself the moral law, which is our basis for belief in God, freedom, and immortality. Therefore, scientific knowledge, morality, and religious belief are mutually consistent and secure because they all rest on the same foundation of human autonomy, which is also the final end of nature according to the teleological worldview of reflecting judgment that Kant introduces to unify the theoretical and practical parts of his philosophical system.[15]

Now, this human activity was split into a different binary than the sacred-secular, into theology and natural religion, which was the positionality within the university as it moved into the 19th century and the modern era of university development.

As noted by Alfred North Whitehead above, the overall effect of philosophy in organizing knowledge differs from religion and science in the West. Enlightenment philosophy changed how to study "religion" in the ways noted above, but the effects of religion and science as organizing principles for knowledge mirror each other. In the West, both religion as formed in Christianity and science as formed by Enlightenment philosophy into empirical science begin with experience and move towards formulation; the former in the formal beliefs expressed in doctrines and creeds, while the latter from hypothesis to theory to the phrase "accepted by the scientific community." In the university location, when in the epistemological position as organizing principles both lean towards producing a hegemonic epistemological lens through which to view the other and philosophy.

This represents an interdisciplinary positionality as our attention shifts to the development of the sacred and profane as the core concept in the academic study of religion as it arose from 19th century linguistics through social science, into the 20th century as the History of Religions project to develop a science of religions, and into the critiques of that project that arose in the latter parts of the 20th century and continued here in the 21st. While there are many players and positions in the narrative, Mircea Eliade and the social constructionist critiques, especially of Russell McCutcheon, embody characteristics of this historical development that assist in the interdisciplinary development of a new space for knowledge production.

Something other than an "and" or an "is"   55

Emile Durkheim's 19th-century articulation of the sacred and profane, while for him pertaining to the activities of social groups, Christianity in particular, established the foundation for the trajectory of the modern study of religion through another re-presentation of the conceptual construction of a two-world domain:

> All known religious beliefs, whether simple or complex, present one common characteristic: they presuppose a classification of all the things, real and ideal, of which men think, into two classes or opposed groups, generally designated by two distinct terms which are translated well enough by the words profane and sacred [profane, *sacré*]. This division of the world into two domains, the one containing all that is sacred, the other all that is profane, is the distinctive trait of religious thought; the beliefs, myths, dogmas and legends are either representations or systems of representations which express the nature of sacred things, the virtues and powers which are attributed to them, or their relations with each other and with profane things.[16]

Eliade integrated Rudolf Otto's phenomenological concept of the *mysterium tremendum* to set the stage of the century's discussion, declaring that "the first possible definition of the *sacred* is that it is *the opposite of the profane*"[17] and "that *sacred* and *profane* are two modes of being in the world, two existential situations assumed by man . . . the *sacred* and *profane* modes of being depend upon the different positions that man has conquered in the cosmos . . ."[18] Thus, the foundation of his work was maintaining Durkheim's opposition of the sacred to, though ironically Eliade would spend his academic career chronicling the instances of boundary violations of this opposition.

Eliade held that in phenomena involving an encounter of human being with the domain of the sacred there appears an irreducible element of human experience that epistemological constructions out of the university disciplinary silos do not account for:

> A religious phenomenon will only be recognized as such if it is grasped at its own level, that is to say, if it is studied *as* something religious. To try to grasp the essence of such phenomenon by means of physiology, psychology, sociology, economics, linguistics, art or any other study is false; it misses the one unique and irreducible element in it – the element of the sacred.[19]

He had identified a reductionism that the university's epistemology, organized as it is by science, tends towards. The social and natural sciences had camouflaged a portion of human experience that the History of Religions'

56 *Something other than an "and" or an "is"*

philosophical phenomenology had uncovered, unencumbered by what modern science was increasingly doing to knowledge formation:

> For the philosophy of science that has emerged since the mid-nineteenth century as the heir of the theory of knowledge is methodology pursued with a scientistic self-understanding of the sciences. "Scientism" means science's belief in itself; that is, the conviction that we can longer understand science as one form of possible knowledge, but rather must identify knowledge with science . . . But by making a dogma of the sciences' belief in themselves, positivism assumes the prohibitive function of protecting scientific inquiry from epistemological self-reflection. Positivism is philosophical only insofar as is necessary for the immunization of the sciences against philosophy.[20]

Uncovered by philosophical phenomenology Eliade proceeded to establish how the appearance of this in human activity can be categorized and classified:

> Man becomes aware of the sacred because it manifests itself, shows itself, as something wholly different from the profane. To designate the *act of manifestation* of the sacred, we have proposed the term *hierophany*. It is a fitting term, because it does not imply anything further; it expresses no more than is implicit in its etymological content, i.e., that *something sacred shows itself to us*. It could be said that the history of religions – from the most primitive to the most highly developed – is constituted by a great number of hierophanies, by manifestations of sacred realities.[21]

Eliade justified his viewpoint in part by positing something in the structure of human consciousness that accounted for the appearance of the sacred in human life. Some aspect of an encounter with certain objects and/or persons, the immersion in events or processes, even features of the physical world triggered this part of human consciousness. It was a universal aspect of human being, with the historical detailing of how this encounter appeared in various cultures and eras becoming the epistemological task. Scholars could study that response as part of a larger science of religions, the 20th century's History of Religions as a disciplinary endeavor within the university.

But, by the end of the 20th century this great university project showed fissures. Eliade and the Chicago School were reproached for their own "particular kind of reductionism . . . aptly called . . . pietistic reductionism (or, alternatively, 'sacred reductionism' or 'enchanted reductionism') [which] treats the religious traditions and developments in the religious world as

Something other than an "and" or an "is" 57

though they were politically/ideologically neuter."[22] Furthermore, the whole prospect of developing a science of religions – complete with a necessarily universal object of study and disciplinary methodologies to classify and categorize its occurrence – met with contention.

Alongside the historicizing of the concept of religion, the notion that Eliade and others were capturing an essential and universal aspect of humanity was relativized. Eliade was critiqued as harboring a hidden, maybe unintentional theology, but one surely shaped by his Western, Eastern European location. Eliade was critiqued for how his personal background had shaped what he saw and how he saw it; he bore personal political preunderstandings into his professional projects naively unaware at best, nefarious at worst.

And those critiques were summarized best by Russell McCutcheon's social constructionist declaration that "by eliminating Mircea Eliade's conjunction 'and' in his well-known title, *The Sacred and the Profane: The Nature of Religion*, we intend to dispel the notion that these two designators name separate domains that somehow interact from time to time."[23] Historicizing designators like "sacred" and "profane," as well as the more commonly used "religion" and "religious," McCutcheon and others persuasively argued that without a historical consciousness the academic study of religion fails to grasp how history has shaped understandings of its basic concepts as they were conceived and used to build its line of inquiry in the latter part of the 20th century. This is especially true of Eliade and others who, like him, advocate a view of "sui generis religion [which involves] excluding sociopolitical analysis from much scholarship on religion."[24]

But of course, historical understandings are incomplete without considering how knowledge developed as it has in the university location. In the early 21st century conversation in religious studies turned towards the prospect that it could not fit into the scientific design of the modern university's knowledge "gathering strategies" and "ordering formations." More and more it was becoming evident to some that the epistemological project of the *universitas*, in its allegiance to the gathering of knowledge through increased specialization, disciplinary knowledge silos, and the unitary ordering of scientism, would exclude a "scientific study of religion." Thus, it was in the tone of a lament that the pursuit of a science of religions appeared impossible and with resignation that the prospect of studying human being, being religious needed to be offered back to other university disciplines, excluding of course theology, which carried its allegiances so visibly on its sleeve.

> Our first assumption is that the modern western research university is a purpose-designed institution for obtaining knowledge about the world . . . [and] is successful only when it is not in service of ideologi-

58   *Something other than an "and" or an "is"*

cal, theological, and religious agendas. Rather, its primary objective is scientific, that is, to gain public (intersubjectively available) knowledge of public (intersubjectively available) facts . . . We now understand that we were both deluded by our overly optimistic but cognitively naïve expectations for the development of a truly scientific field for the study of religion in the context of a modern, research university.[25]

And as the social constructionist critique historicized the sacred and profane as the 20th century's History of Religions project had conceptualized them, it was still not without its own evidence of the influence of disciplinary yields. Ironically, as Eliade's quest began with a critique of the reductionism of disciplinary pursuits and ended with the countercharges of the social constructionists who are

> in tension on a number of theoretical and methodological issues . . . [they] *share* at least one common feature: both are interested in delimiting the bounds of an other (the reductionist in the first case [Eliade], the liberal humanist in the second [social constructionist]), who is stuck in the past, as a way of validating their own projects, headed as they are to a better future.[26]

For our interdisciplinary purposes there are several useful returns on the historical development of religious studies within the epistemological project that is the modern university. First, that what an unsystematic thinker like Eliade leaves us with is not a concern for concepts, "but rather the way these two are actually experienced . . . [that is] the phenomenological method that claims to describe these experience of the sacred and profane."[27] In other words, our interest is how concepts can be used as descriptive interpretation of the function of human activity. Secondly, as social constructionist critique suggest, the delimiting of the concepts of the sacred and profane, and religious and secular, prohibit their use in projecting them back into history to understand the actions of ancient cultures and peoples. The sacred especially denotes no thing, no universality, but is only useful as a historically developed concept. Ironically, in an epistemological location organized by science and tending to value phenomena that can be universally categorized, it should be no surprise that "the universality of religion tends to be taken as a given in most academic departments."[28] Which brings us to the third useful yield. The mirrored reductionisms of the History of Religionists and the social constructionists might portend something else and other. If the study of religion in the university location circumscribed today by science, and some say scientism, as its epistemological organizing principle, characterized by the fruits of disciplinarity – soiled knowledge, specialization, and reductionism – then perhaps religious

Something other than an "and" or an "is"   59

studies is fertile ground for an interdisciplinary style whereby knowledge is produced in a space in-between the disciplines, not by concepts established in the university being confirmed by engaging activity outside the university, but transformed. There may be a way of conceiving religious activity as world-building and yet, not building the world.

Something other in the production of an additional domain

It can be noted that in the generation of the concepts of the sacred and profane by Durkheim in the late 1800s, he was standing in the lineage of philosophy's Enlightenment division of its inherited understanding of religion into the theology and natural religion. The sacred and profane's parentage is the philosophical product, natural religion. It can also be noted that in social constructionism's collapse of the sacred and profane, it returned the conceptual foundation of study to its earliest university form, the Augustinian single domain of the human existence as the singular existential domain of the City of God and City of Man. But there are further implications that can be drawn.

That the central concepts do not possess the universality of history and culture that a disciplinary epistemic structure maintains they do or should, and as the unitary organizing principles of the modern university, science, are insufficient for the field of study, is evidence of the limits of knowledge gathering siloed by disciplinarity, and knowledge ordering by science alone. This condition offers an "establishing [of] a kind of undisciplined space in the interstices between disciplines,"[29] providing the opportunity to integrate "the insights of knowledge domains to produce a more comprehensive understanding of complex problems, issues, or questions [drawn from] real world applications."[30]

In his *Why the World Does Not Exist*, philosopher Markus Gabriel seeks to dispel a common misconception: that the world exists. The world is not the universe, "the experimentally accessible OBJECT DOMAIN of the natural sciences,"[31] which can measure and can account for the universe. The world is larger than the universe because the world contains thoughts and imaginings and memories that no scientific, empirical rule can account for.

> One might think that the world is the domain of all those things that simply exist without our assistance and that surround us in this way . . . If the world is really absolutely everything, then governments, dreams [of every single person], unrealized possibilities, works of art, and notably our thoughts about the world also belong to it. Thus, a good number of objects exist which man cannot touch . . . [Even] Our thoughts about the world remain in the world . . . The question is never simply whether

60 *Something other than an "and" or an "is"*

something exists but always *where* something exists. For everything that exists, exists somewhere – even if is only in our imagination. Again, the one exception is the world. This we cannot imagine at all.[32]

Everything exists in a location and, thus, there is no rule or set of rules organized objectively from data gathered, that constitutes the world though in the intellectual history of the West "one explorer of an alleged world formula has followed the next for almost three thousand years: from Thales of Miletus to Karl Marx and Stephen Hawking."[33] The universe may be accounted for but still, the larger world is not and therefore does not exist. Even though we may talk about it.

And the world is also not just the construction of it from a location. The world as constituted of just locational construction "claims we cannot know the rule . . . [and] while we attempt to reach an agreement about which illusion we want to be applied, we find ourselves entangled in power struggle or communicative actions."[34] We construct some knowledge, true, and some worlds, true again, from brain receptors receiving stimuli from outside, and we do construct interpretations, and while

> the concept of a fact and the concept of knowledge are connected in diverse ways . . . no analysis of this connection should lead to the false result that there exist no facts but only interpretations, and consequently the analysis, at some point, must likewise be erroneous.[35]

Universalizing the sacred implies imagining a world from no particular location, *an inclusive all locations*, which really is not a world that exists. Universalizing renders the concept useless. Likewise, collapsing and reducing the sacred to the profane, to one particularized location that is constructed – culture and history – is no less useful. "By CONSTUCTIVISM I understand the assumption that 'we cannot discover any fact 'in itself,' but have instead constructed all facts ourselves."[36]

The world doesn't exist because we cannot imagine it but only as domains. Gabriel notes a failure in the modern university as an epistemological project conceiving knowledge as organized by the empirical sciences in search of the universe's metaphysical rules revealing the order of the world, or political science and cultural critique positing that all worlds are interpretations and constructions:

> both metaphysics and constructivism fail because of an unjustified simplification of reality, in which they understand reality unilaterally either as *the world without spectators* or, equally one-sided, as *the world of spectators* . . . The world is neither exclusively the world without spectators nor the world of spectators.[37]

Something other than an "and" or an "is"   61

One way to identify interdisciplinarity as a positionality is to distinguish it from other "extra-disciplinary" forms of epistemological assemblages: "*Multidisciplinarity* [has been] defined as an approach that juxtaposes disciplines . . . foster[ing] wider knowledge, information, and methods."[38] While multidisciplinarity can be "defined as an approach that juxtaposes disciplines . . . integration of disciplines [is] the 'litmus test' of interdisicplinarity."[39] Thus, interdisciplinarity might assist us in taking the concepts from inside the university location outside of it to encounter certain moments as they are experienced; heightened moments like when a person is moving from the land of the living to the land of the dead, a moment within the profane domain of a hospital operating room and on the cusp of a sacred domain which human religious activity posits as not the living, material world but an addition beyond or behind it. But the conceptual domains in the university – argued as the sacred and the profane – do not circumscribe the domain that is being experienced in the sensations generated there. It is a space in-between university-devised domains and more like a space that is simultaneously identical with other ordinary times and places in a world where thousands die each day, and extraordinary in its features of a particular life moving into death; like

> between the flame and its burning power, or the musk and its smell, the relations between . . . the source and the emanation . . . [the] seeming paradox [that] can take place on the level of consciousness, which is free from the limitations of . . . logical distinctions . . . [which as] simultaneous difference and nondifference, can be conceived of in the consciousness, and can therefore exist.[40]

In the modern university, scholars in the physics department can generate rules regarding energy and the transformation and transference of it when wood is consumed by flame. In the modern university, scholars in cultural studies and political science can analyze the power dynamics of gender and economics when a single mother's small home is destroyed and she risks her life saving her only daughter. But neither constitutes the world any more than the profane and the sacred are complete domains either unto themselves or collapsed into one. When you are sitting with that mother in the heightened moment of a life passing into death as all lives do, her body charred almost beyond recognition and lying prone and still on a hospital gurney, in the chilly and shiny and bare hospital room where you sit beside her in a single chair, you are alone and you are together. She may hear one last thing before she dies but you don't know whether she can or has already slipped past consciousness and towards death. So you tell her what you know, that the daughter she tried to rescue will survive and you promise her that the spiritual community that houses you both will help raise her. And the tear

62   *Something other than an "and" or an "is"*

coming down her check is the only confirmation you can surmise that she might have heard, might know she is being recognized.

There exists something more and other than particularized locations, particularized constructions of the world in that the fact of death, of passing from life into death is not subject to interpretation or variation from location. Yet, we are all located somewhere in that though we can understand how fire operates as part of the physical universe, there is no world we can imagine where we can know that mother's thoughts. And for scholars who study religion we need to remember that while human religious activity might surmise rules governing what "the sacred" is and universalize it, and we as scholars can analyze activity for the cultural and political worlds that are constructed as the profane, we are not studying experience outside the scholar's study and the university's disciplinary structures. We might account for how human religious activity posits a sacred world after the living one or a metaphysical one or "no one" behind the façade of the living one, and we might see how activity constructs in the profane, ordinary world political worlds of power and oppression encased in interpretations of the sacred.

And yet there is also an interdisciplinary positionality that seeks to generate a space in-between what the modern university disciplinary structure discovers and constructs, a space other than or in addition to the domains of the sacred and profane. We have acknowledged that knowledge is shaped by location and is involved in situatedness, and that location is formed by personal and professional history, and all that James identified as what could be attributable to the wider Self. And positionality constitutes an interpretive stance given one's location and situatedness, how we are constructing knowledge out of human activity at certain moments in time while occupying bounded and particular space; that is, residing as we do for as long as we do, in domains.

In looking back and describing and analyzing those moments, we construct from sensations a framework of understanding with students in a classroom; attempting as best all of you can an evaluation of how activity functioned using an interdisciplinary retooling of the classic conceptual two-world domain designators of the sacred and profane; and developing a framework as outsiders (all now) to understand the experience of residing with others as insiders in a new space, an overlapping domain – the sacred-profane. A tear could be from anything, as the medical doctors said the brain registered no feeling, no pain; but pain is more than a phenomenon of the brain because there are more pains than just physical ones. Eliade spent a lifetime chronicling what he called the "sacred irrupting in the profane," a transcendent crashing into the imminent, but here is the memory of a heightened ordinary – which because of its extremity, and the imminence of

Something other than an "and" or an "is" 63

death, the end of residing within the passage of time and movement through space – was not still the profane and not yet the sacred, or whatever transcends, goes beyond what we can see and feel here. Call it an imminent-transcendent, full of the profane of the hospital and death, and still not yet fully the sacred; the phenomenon of residing in an overlapping domain, the sacred-profane. Disoriented and dislocated, the only two things I remember was the chill and brightness of the room and the metal table upon which she lied motionless. And just as memorable, after whispering in her ear, the tear forming out of the corner of an eye hidden by closed and charred eyelids, and rolling down the side of her face.

Notes

1 William James, 1961, pp. 35–36, 301.
2 Ibid., p. 36.
3 Jonathan Z. Smith, 1998, p. 270.
4 Philip Gorski and Ates Altinordu, 2008, p. 60.
5 R. A. Markus, 1970, p. 59.
6 Ibid., p. 122.
7 Ibid., pp. 122–123.
8 Gilles Deleuze and Felix Guattari, 1994, pp. 19–20.
9 Markus, 1970, pp. 122–123.
10 Roland H. Bainton, 1962, p. 138.
11 David Morris, 2004, p. 130.
12 Alister McGrath, 2007, p. 2.
13 Ryan Gillespie, 2014, p. 4.
14 Joe Moran, 2002, p. 9.
15 Michael Rohlf, 2016. Retrieved at: https://plato.stanford.edu/entries/kant/
16 Emile Durkheim, 1915, p. 37.
17 Mircea Eliade, 1957, p. 10.
18 Ibid., pp. 14–15.
19 Mircea Eliade, 1996, p. xiii.
20 Jurgen Habermas, 1971, pp. 4, 67.
21 Ibid., p. 11.
22 Neil McMullins, 1989, pp. 80–96.
23 William E. Arnal and Russell T. McCutcheon, 2013, p. xi.
24 Russell T. McCutcheon, 1997, p. 27.
25 Luther H. Martin and Donald Wiebe, 2014, p. 1129.
26 Benjamin Y. Fong, 2014, p. 1129.
27 Allan W. Larsen, 2001, pp. 49–50.
28 Jason Ananda Josephson, 2012, pp. 2–3.
29 Moran, 2002, p. 15.
30 Preamble, "Association for Interdisciplinary Studies." Retrieved at: https://oakland.edu/ais/about/mission/
31 Markus Gabriel, 2015, p. 8.
32 Ibid., pp. 8–9, 13–14.
33 Ibid., p. 11.
34 Ibid.

64 *Something other than an "and" or an "is"*

35 Ibid., p. 44.
36 Ibid., p. 39.
37 Ibid., p. 7.
38 Julie Thompson Klein, 2010, p. 17.
39 Ibid.
40 Edward C. Dimock, Jr., 1989, p. 163.

3 Sighting the sacred unseen
A camouflaged order appears

Virtual reality environments (VREs) are used in exposure therapy in particular situations. Placing persons with PTSD in a specially designed VRE, or persons on the high functioning end of the autism spectrum in a different but specially designed VRE, alters their condition such that after emerging into the world outside the VRE a measurable change occurs.[1] Because of the immersive quality of the VRE experience, and the sense of presence it generates in persons while they are there, there is an effect that lasts after exiting the ordered world of the VRE. The order affects insiders' sense of self, identity, and their relationship to the world. Paul Ricouer's treatment of the concept of recognition might assist us in understanding more fully the implications of this. He notes a range of the word's meanings. In the active voice, to recognize becomes a mode of knowing: "To recognize as an act expresses a pretension, a claim, to exercise an intellectual mastery over this field of meanings, of signifying assertions."[2] Thus, the VRE insider masters the new order by recognizing in it aspects of the seen, ordinary, profane one the insider exited temporarily. Yet, the effect of immersion and the sense of presence in a new order is just as deep and the passive voice captures this: "the demand for recognition expresses an expectation that can be satisfied only by mutual recognition, where this mutual recognition either remains an unfulfilled dream or requires procedures and institutions that elevate recognition to the political plane."[3] The insider is recognized in return. Imagine a room of students where a teacher asks a question and five hands raise to give an answer. The students have recognized the answer (the active voice of recognition), and when the teacher calls on one, recognition (in the passive voice) has been received.

This is the symbiotic nature of the sacred, unseen order resided in by Christian insiders in communion and Hindu insiders in Ganges River bathing. An interdisciplinarity approach takes scholars to the site of each, particular as each is within different traditions and specific as the events are within those traditions, armed with both disciplinary yields and the need to

66 *Sighting the sacred unseen*

integrate those to produce a creative hermeneutic out of the uniqueness of this encounter. The scholar is interpreting how activity functions for insiders as they reside in the sacred-profane domain, where experiences with objects become manifestations of that domain that generate a sacred, unseen order in which persons and communities are fully immersed with a sense of presence that changes them. They reside in the sacred/profane and emerged affected by having been recognized.

Thus in summary, using the characteristics of an interdisciplinary approach in religious studies that designates the sacred/profane as a new domain engaged in by insiders and displaying the characteristics of simultaneity, residence, and immersion which yields an experience distinctive to the insider characterized by Ricouer's notion of "being recognized," we can see how insider activity responds to that recognition by the creation of an unseen order of time and space – unseen, that is, by the outsider/scholar – within which insiders reside. Thus, religious studies scholars are studying how insider activity functions to establish and maintain residence in this sacred/profane, unseen order that generates a distinctive kind of experience denoted by the concept of the hierophany. The analogy of the VRE helps us to understand more deeply how this insider activity functions. While inside of the sacred/profane domain insiders take up an immersive residence in an order of time and space that simultaneously overlaps with the order of time and space insiders share with outsiders who are observing. While the outsider shares with the insider the profane, cultural quality of the objects and processes, the outsider is observing insider residence in an order that is simultaneously sacred and profane by virtue of insider generative and responsive activity that has an immersive effect.

An interdisciplinary approach allows a retooling of the concept of the unseen order as a domain experienced by insiders. Through a parallax history of the concept, the neglect of this concept by university epistemological processes is apparent. The birth of religious studies from its parental lineage in theology and the social sciences gave it a suspicion of one, theology, and an inability to shake how the social sciences were shaped by science as the university's organizing principle. It was not until the advent of digital technology that scholars could experience an unseen order in a first-order and second-order way that was outside of considerations of meaning that are at the heart of theology. And in the case of the use of exposure therapy the effects of immersive residence in that order yielded a transfer from the unseen order of the insider participant to the seen, profane, everyday order shared with outsider non-participants. Immersive residence inside of two orders simultaneously can be understood by the theologian relative to the substantive meaning of that residence and explained by computer science and the health sciences in terms of the effects of virtual environments on

Sighting the sacred unseen 67

human physiology and behavior. Even philosophy weighs in concerning the concept of human nature. And readers will also enlarge their understanding that through generating an interdisciplinary lens, religious studies, the activity by insiders in the sacred/profane domain, can be understood as it functions to generate an unseen order that exhibits simultaneity in insider immersive residence.

Abstract

In his *The Varieties of Religious Experience*, William James described "the religious attitude" as "the belief that there is an unseen order, and that our supreme good lies in harmoniously adjusting ourselves thereto."[4] While James' approach has been determined as incomplete, his concept of the "unseen order" has received much less attention. This paper will use religious studies as an interdisciplinary enterprise to retool the concept of the "unseen order." Recent advances in technology and the emergence of digital studies give new impetus to retooling it. The "unseen order" can become a useful concept for analyzing and understanding human religious behavior as generative of a sacred domain within which insiders reside whilst simultaneously residing in a seen, profane domain shared with the scholar outsider. What retooling suggests is that domains like the sacred and profane are neither opposing (Eliade) nor corresponding (social constructionism). With the prominence of cinema, and the emergence of video gaming and immersive virtual reality environments something beyond either is suggested. These technologically produced domains give the academic study of religion a practical 21st-century activity expressing characteristics of a conceptual tool that has lain dormant for most of the previous century.

Text

Residing in an unseen order

For my class "Religion and Popular Culture" we visit our new library built as an information and technology center because as is the case with any university, student laptops contain more access to ordered information and text than any university. We go into the Technology Showcase, a single room where students can experience the latest technological iterations including augmented reality, 3D printers, and virtual reality. Each student compliments the previous week's work studying the history of the concepts of the sacred/profane and the unseen order, with a dive into a VRE. Most students have never experienced these and are surprised how utterly different and exponentially more complex they are than watching a movie, a video on a

68 *Sighting the sacred unseen*

computer screen, playing a video game at home, or using a computer generated simulator. VREs offer residence in an ordered world.

A VRE "integrates real-time computer graphics, body-tracking devices, visual displays, and other sensory input devices to immerse a participant in a computer-generated virtual environment that changes in a natural way with head and body motion."[5] Each distinctive VRE is

> an advanced form of human–computer interaction that allows the user to "interact" with computers and digital content in a more natural or sophisticated fashion relative to what is afforded by standard mouse and keyboard input devices. Immersive VR can be produced by combining computers, head-mounted displays (HMDs), body-tracking sensors, specialized interface devices, and real-time graphics to immerse a participant in a computer-generated simulated world that changes in a natural/intuitive way with head and body motion.[6]

Each student is immersed inside of a domain ordered in time and space in such a way that it generates for them a sense of presence in that domain, which remains unseen to the other student "outsiders." For insiders it is the ordered domain of their residence; and yet, for insiders the VRE domain functions as an overlapping domain with the Technology Showcase room shared with outsiders. Put on VR goggles and move about physically as residing inside of a domain of space and time that responds to your actions and is unseen by others, and still you might bump into the chairs that outsiders are sitting on in the room. Residing in the overlap of two domains can have startling effects as in the use of VREs in exposure therapy.[7] Understanding how overlapping domains function involve "approaches to knowledge [that] emphasize the irreducible complexity of phenomena, often embedded [as they are] in systems characterized by multiple nexus points of interaction."[8]

In his *The Varieties of Religious Experience*, William James described "the religious attitude" as "the belief that there is an unseen order, and that our supreme good lies in harmoniously adjusting ourselves thereto."[9] In the more than a century since James' declaration, his study has accumulated a large body of critique but his concept of the "unseen order" has received scant attention.[10] Instead, ocularcentrism occupies Western interests as it has for thousands of years, from the time persons emerged into the light from the shadows of Plato's cave, to God's all-seeing powers, and the "apparent non-interference of vision with the world it perceives [allowed] the formation of the notion of objectivity and thought that exists independently of that which it perceives . . ."[11] It is what can be seen that is prominent even though we are immersed in the invisible and the unseen, the "many forms of invisibility . . . [from] myths and folklore . . . [to] fierce commentaries on injustice . . . [to] forced invisibility . . . in our society . . . [to] the dead [who]

Sighting the sacred unseen 69

are presently absent and, through memory, absently present,"[12] and "understanding of the invisible has also been an important topic in the study and theories of human development"[13] in part because "invisibility works in our meaning making and dynamic construction of ourselves in relation to others."[14] We are shaped by what we cannot see as much as what we can and do, and considering what it means to reside inside the invisible "de-objectif[ies] and de-reif[ies] sight [and] emphasize[s] the spontaneous participation of the whole body and all the senses in perception."[15]

When my students visit the library's Technology Showcase they are both observing another residing inside what is to them an unseen order and then when it is their turn, they step into a structured order of time and space they had not before seen, and in more sophisticated VREs, perform seeing, hearing, and even smelling as part of insider sensorial response.

In other words, in the experience of stepping into a VRE, a hitherto unseen order, human beings gain access to another structured order of time and place that, while exhibiting features of the ordinary order of the everyday which generate sensorial response, compose an alternate yet overlapping context with the ordinary everyday. We are observing an old activity which we long ago assigned a concept to, reflex action, being "that the acts we perform are always the result of outward discharges from the nervous centres, and that these outward discharges are themselves the result of impressions from the external world, carried in along one or another of ours sensory nerves."[16] What "residing" means as a description of the condition of ontological location and action – Heidegger's "'being in the world' [in] Merleau-Ponty's . . . view [that] the world of objects is not something apart from us as subjects, acting upon us causally, but the place we *inhabit* . . . the inseparability of subject and world"[17] – is on fuller display not because of a change of ontology but of location. Thus, our considerations involve the features of the interaction between insiders and location as inseparable and dynamic, displayed when the order that makes location, location, changes. The irony shouldn't be lost on any instructor familiar with the metaphysical faux text question: Describe the universe and give two examples. As analogy – similarity-in-difference – is a critical component in interpretation, we have here an analogy that can retool the concept of the unseen order as not just useful but invaluable in performing an interdisciplinary style of religious studies methodology. After leaving the university study, at the location of human activity, the self-conscious interdisciplinary religious studies scholar engages insiders residing in a sacred unseen order overlapping the ordinary seen order shared by both. The difference is twofold. Insiders reside in one structured order of time and place the scholar does not. And, insider activity generates the unseen order to which insiders respond both while residing in the sacred unseen order and upon return to the ordinary world of shared sight with the scholar.

70 *Sighting the sacred unseen*

Residing in an unseen order

Invisibility can be the function of a whole host of conditions such as location in not having the sight lines to see an object, or society in terms of extending rights, or even movement when you slowly walk down a street you've driven by a thousand times and glimpse houses you hadn't noticed. Invisibility involves the liquid you put behind the ears in the case of perfume, the garlic in your squash soup, the distant sound of a clocktower at noon, and the heat off of your sick child's forehead as you reach down to check their status. And seeing the depth of the space around us and within which we are insiders, as "an already given space, characterized apart from the living activity of the body"[18] is to engage in what is called the "'experience error'";[19] that is, the error of seeing my child's room from the "my-own" vantage point as containing objective space inhabited by an *other* constituted by my neurological processes of cognition to be a part of this space, but a space that, unbeknownst to me is absent of the me included in the affectional possessive, *my* child. "Our sense of space is not constituted by cognitive or neurobiological structures that are merely on our side of things; our sense of space is enfolded in an outside, in a world that crosses our body."[20] Each of the instances of invisibility above involve a context human beings are immersed in and where we gain our sense of presence as structured by time, formed in space, and directed through intention as "being-in-the-world . . . our ways of being involved with the world, the purposes we have in relation to surrounding objects and the meanings that we give to them . . . in the *social* and *cultural* worlds as well as in the world of physical nature."[21]

There's no location that encompasses all locations and the world is more than what I see from my location as the space containing *my* child. Treating a location as a domain without a sensing human being packing a point of view, or as a domain with only what a sensing human being's point of view unpacks, neglects the dynamic we are immersed in when we view the world from a standing where we cannot see ourselves or only see ourselves. Residing in a VRE and the Technology Showcase makes prominent this realization. "The world is neither exclusively the world without spectators nor the world of spectators."[22] Writes neurobiologist and cognitive scientist David Presti in *Mind Beyond Brain*, "While the existence of a 'real' world external to us is extrapolated and assumed, we only come to know this assumed objective world via our experience. *There is an inextricable enfolding of mind and world.*"[23] And when you move about in a VRE concurrently with the Technology Showcase room itself, you are existing in a peculiar form of simultaneity: overlapping domains, the simultaneous identify and difference of time, space, and intention.

Sighting the sacred unseen   71

Residing in time in an unseen order

As "our experience of space has been utterly transformed by technological advances . . . enhancing the significance of space,"[24] so has our understanding of time. We talk about our "sense of time" even though "time is not a true sense such as vision or hearing [as we possess] no organ of time . . . Nevertheless, the brain not only measures time, but it senses the passage of time, we seem to feel time flow."[25] In *Felt Time: The Science of How We Experience Time*, psychologist Marc Wittman notes all the various ways we measure time and duration, from today as "embedded between two phases of rest that constitute a natural border of time"[26] to the university construct of the academic year. "Just as cultures may be distinguished in terms of political, economic, and historical factors, they can be defined in terms of how time is managed and subjectively experienced."[27] In 1999, Zimbardo and Boyd first named these as Time Perspectives: "the often non-conscious process whereby the continual flows of personal and social experiences are assigned to temporal categories, or time frames, that help to give order, coherence, and meaning to those events."[28] The lived body is not "merely manifest in time, it is *of* temporality, in the way that the lived body is not in space, but *of* it . . ."[29]

And the effect of residing in ordered time and space is noticeable when observing persons residing in overlapping Time Perspective domains such as is the case during a futbol match. Spectators and athletes both reside in the Time Perspective domains of culture and contest, though in different ways. How much more so, then, when the overlapping domains involve worlds? When students step out of the VRE they routinely report having to reorient themselves in terms of how much time is left in class. They return into the ordinary, profane domain but in that passage need an adjustment of their sense of time. Curiously they routinely call this a return to "reality" or "the real world," marking off a distinction with the world as ordered outside the VRE. Residing in the overlap of two orders of time and space, two worlds occupied simultaneously, creates a new space for knowledge production, the overlapping Time Perspective domain that resists a reductionistic description from either of the separate domains.

The study of the human condition inside a VRE rests largely on two concepts: immersion and sense of presence:

> [P]resence in a VE is inherently a function of the user's psychology, representing the extent to which an individual experiences the virtual setting as the one in which they are consciously present . . . [Whereas] immersion can be regarded as a quality of the system's technology, an objective measure of the extent to which the system presents a vivid virtual environment while shutting out physical reality.[30]

72   Sighting the sacred unseen

Sense of presence is the psychological identification by the individual of their "belongingness" to the domain the VRE creates, that they reside inside the orders of time and place making up the unseen order invisible to others. It is the "defining aspect of the virtual experience."[31] Immersion is the quality of the domain itself as an experience of ordered time and place that is responsive to the adaptations and creative initiatives the insider undertakes; that is, the way the domain is structured so as *to receive* and *be responsive to* the activities of insiders. It is a quality of the order or world within which insiders are located that would add immeasurably to our understandings of the dynamism whereby a particular time and place imprints itself upon insiders.[32] Sense of presence and immersion are concepts used to understand the dynamic interaction between human being and the world as functions of time and place.

In VREs a sense of presence is more powerful emotionally the more insiders reside in the order as an environment that is "not mediated by technology . . . [but is a] comparable life situation . . . [supporting] the notion that presence levels are related to the level of experienced emotions."[33] Used in exposure therapy to treat persons with PTSD, for example, the VRE is structured in terms of time and place to reproduce activity that generated the trauma. This gives insiders the opportunity to generate new memories through simultaneity, residing in overlapping domains; the sense of presence in the threatening time and place of a past battlefield and the sense of presence in the time and place of the current security of home.

Insiders are engaging an event in addition to the memory of their traumatic event, but the engagement is not as though the insiders are objects among other objects composing a past moment. Neither is it the case that the "experience cannot contain its structure or form *in itself*, [and] that it can have such structure only if our minds impose it upon a formless matter of sensation."[34] Instead, there is an intimate involvement that generates a strong sense of presence. Insiders reside in a "virtual world that is as similar as possible to the real-world environment in which the traumatic event occurred"[35] including sights, sounds, smells, touch (feel of vibration), and the capacity for insider movement within a location structured as the past event. In the duration of their residence in certain VREs designed for an emotional effect, "different VEs may be used to induce specific emotional states"[36] that in the case of their use with persons with PTSD and certain anxiety disorders, can produce distinctive and intentional effects when insiders return to the ordinary world. This tells us something about the nature of residing in overlapping domains as structured orders of time.

The sense of presence generated by residing in overlapping domains, simultaneously residing in both a past threat and a present security as in the case of PTSD treatment, or a future security and a present threat as in

Sighting the sacred unseen 73

anxiety disorders, mimics what modern physics says about how we reside in time in the ordinary order of our everyday, called presentism, and time as structured in existence which holds us, called eternalism. Human experience of time overlaps with the metaphysical structure of time. Ordinarily we reside in this moment, with a future of moments yet to be and a past of moments that have occurred but are gone, like the event that precipitated the trauma of the person with PTSD or the anxiety reduced events of the future for those with anxiety disorders. Described as such, presentism involves the manner in which the brain creates a flow to the time of events:

> We can say that we measure duration with a clock. But to do so requires us to read it at two different moments: this is not possible, because we are always in one moment, never in two. In the present, we see only the present; we can see things that we interpret as traces of the past, but there is a categorical difference between seeing *traces* of the past and perceiving the flow of time – and Augustine realizes that the root of this difference, the awareness of the passing of time, is internal. It is the traces left in the brain by the past.[37]

From the standpoint of time as the brain ordinarily makes sense of it, the person with PTSD can be characterized as being captured by the traces of a past event. From the presentism's understanding of time reliving the event would only compound the trauma. You can't change the past. But, as residing inside a VRE is residing in overlapping domains of time, the moment of the past and the moment of the present are experienced simultaneously, and the past threatening event, which contained no security, is now experienced in an overlap with the secure domain of home where taking off the goggles yields familiar faces of loved ones. Linguistic explanations don't quite account for this. From a presentist positionality the traumatic event happened as a past event and only the bad memory bridges the divide. But from the eternalist positionality something different is understood concerning the metaphysical nature of time:

> Language poses a long-standing impediment to unambiguous conversations about presentism and eternalism. For example, words like "real" and "exist" can have very different meanings depending on whether one is speaking under the umbrella of presentism or of eternalism. In the context of presentism, the statement "dinosaurs exist" is false. But under eternalism, one might argue that the statement is true, because dinosaurs do exist at some other moment in time, a moment that is equally real as the moment you consider to be *now* . . . Under presentism *real* means it *exists now* and only *now*, because the present is

74 *Sighting the sacred unseen*

the only moment anything can exist in. In contrast, for an eternalist *real* can refer to something that *exists* anywhere/anywhen within the block universe, including dinosaurs and your future descendants.[38]

We feel time flowing because we construct our world ordinarily as presentists. The present is all we reside in at any given moment, the past is what went on before and is over, the future what might be but is not yet. Our brains construct time like we're watching a movie with frames moving so as to shape it into a reasonable flow with the current scene in relation to the opening credits. Modern physics indicates that existence is metaphysically structured differently in terms of time. Existence is like the film itself, all frames existing simultaneously in the reel we can hold, all the moments simultaneously but which we cannot enjoy and make sense of except by running the reel.

> When a physicist suggests that the flow of time is an illusion, she is suggesting that it exists only in our minds, and that it is not a feature of the external world. When a neuroscientist states that our subjective sense of the passage of time is an illusion, she is suggesting that, like all subjective experiences, it is a mental construct, but one that represents, however unfaithfully, a physical phenomenon that *does* exist in the external world ... Deciphering whether the flow of time is a fiction created by the mind or something that eludes the current laws of physics is a uniquely complex problem that lies at the interface of physics and neuroscience.[39]

The VRE/Technology Showcase residence involves overlapping domains. No wonder then that students are disoriented stepping out of an overlapping Time Perspective domain and back into the *real*, ordinary world where they are in the singular domain of the Technology Showcase with time flowing as it ordinarily does, *having been* in a VRE they are not presently in. The sense of presence is profound and camouflage the overlap. And neither does the scholar who doesn't look for the space in-between the two separate domains.

The function of exposure therapy's healing effects can be explained scientifically. But for the interdisciplinary religious studies scholar a new space has been created for the possibility of knowledge production in the concept of the overlapping domain with its simultaneous residence in two structures of temporality, an overlap of Time Perspectives. When we view religious activity performed by insiders we are studying the function of activities generating a new domain in which insiders reside in time differently structured, their sense of presence residing inside of the new domain of

Sighting the sacred unseen 75

time differently structured, while simultaneously residing inside of ordinary time shared with the scholar. This is an in-between domain generated and resided in. It involves sensations generated by insiders' sense of presence residing in one time domain, the sacred unseen order of how to the insider time is metaphysically structured, simultaneous with a sense of presence in another, the ordinary where time flows in past, present, and future moments shared with the scholar. And the interdisciplinary religious studies scholar is studying this overlapping domain composed when insiders possess a sense of presence in the sacred, unseen domain of time so deeply their immersion involves a sensation not shared with the outside scholar.

Residing in space in an unseen order

The study of VRE offers us an additional concept, immersion, which also characterizes what the interdisciplinary scholar has uncovered as new space in the overlap of two domains. The concept of immersion refers to a quality of the environment to which human beings are symbiotically located when they step into a VRE. Immersion is about place, about the architecture of the VRE. To understand the concept more deeply, immersion is analogous to the relationship between buildings and their inhabitants as studied in architecture. Juhani Pallasmaa proposed that the function of architecture "is to create embodied and lived existential metaphors that concretize and structure our being in the world . . . [and manufacturing] a bodily reaction is an inseparable aspect of the experience of architecture."[40] Immersion in a VRE can be construed as a concept to study how place is structured as an embodiment of existential living receptive to human agency. In exposure therapy VREs are designed to produce a response that aids insiders in the world outside the VRE, a carried over "cash value" aim of what we now can call residence in overlapping domains to be distinguished from explanations as "after-effects";[41] an aim realized if the sense of presence and immersion are so intense insiders will suspend in part the realization of residence in the ordinary shared with the scholar. By knowing the place the VRE constructs and successfully negotiating the activities in that place, insiders gain a new identity in life after the trauma in the case of persons with PTSD and beyond previously held limitations for those with anxiety disorders. And notably in the case of their use with children who are burn victims, residence in the place-architecture of the VRE assists in preparation for treatment beyond what was thought they could endure.[42] The place-architecture of the VRE involves immersion that generates something more.

As residing in a place involves human interaction in and with location, it also involves *space*, "the experience of our situatedness vis-à-vis the body, others and the world about us."[43] And this understanding of space as

76   *Sighting the sacred unseen*

body-situated can be characterized as "neither the cladding of pure subjectivity nor an object in the world; the crossing of body and world turns any simple division of subject and object into a problem," that of a perceiving body that "is not self-contained" residing in a "perceived world [that] is not a self-contained system."[44] To be human is not to reside in a particular place but to move into, about, and through various places resided in and shared with others on earth, "not devoid of place but laden with it."[45]

Immersion refers to the symbiotic nature of environment and organism, places and person and persons, that is, residing as an attribute of our being.

> Our sense of orientation is not rooted in neural structures, a priori intuitions . . . [but in] a way of moving and grasping the world, and in a deep grammar of the body, a topo-logic of a body that can face or not face itself, and thereby (conversely) not face or face others and its place.[46]

Insiders know and come to dwell in any ordered domain by recognition, by what philosopher Paul Ricouer noted is the active voice meaning of the verb *to recognize* as "the initial quasi indistinguishableness of recognizing and knowing"[47] as the process of "distinguish[ing] and identify[ing] . . . which is the act of judging."[48] For the insider this action of coming to know the structured order of, say, a VRE is no different in function and effect than the process of distinguishing and identifying in their knowing the ordinary domain they share with outsiders. In either domain, human beings know through recognition. But in residing simultaneously in an order like a VRE, insiders reside in an additional process of knowing that outsiders do not. And immersion in what the interdisciplinary scholar sees as an overlapping domain can yield sensations not shared by the scholar residing in the ordinary one, sensations that generate knowledge.

This additional and different kind of knowledge is hinted at by David Morgan's work in studying religion and visual culture:

> Apparitions and visions are phenomena in which people report seeing something. Sometimes they describe ocular experiences of things; other occasions suggest more subjective events comparable to dreams or mental occurrences that have no corresponding physical manifestation. But whether staged within or without the brain, people say they saw something.[49]

To the scholar who treats these out of the siloed epistemologies of the university, these sensations could variously be identified and understood neurologically as originating in a part of the brain, or sociologically as the cause of social stigmatization, or categorized psychologically as delusion or illusion

Sighting the sacred unseen 77

or hallucination. The scholar outside the unseen order can use the process of active recognition as knowing, as is performed in the ordinary order of the university scholar. Ricoeur's active voice yields different results based upon disciplinary domain of primary residence. However, the interdisciplinary scholar recognizes insiders as residing in a domain the scholar does not and, hence, can see a prospect that might elude the siloed knowledge of the disciplines. After self-conscious scrutiny of intent, a perquisite for the scholar performing interdisciplinarity in that it will shape knowledge "recognized," the scholar builds a framework of interdisciplinary understanding generated from the recognition of the new space, the overlapping domain. In addition to what the scholar knows of insider activity by active recognition, the scholar also recognizes an epistemological feature of insiders' immersive residing in a domain the scholar is not.

Ricouer part imported from intro for evaluation

And the origin of knowledge is in recognition. Years after my parents retired to Florida and my father had died, I returned to my small town Indiana neighborhood to see the old home only to find a façade that was strangely altered. I only knew it was my childhood home after recognizing it as the second house from the woods, distinguished from the first and third. Philosopher Paul Ricoeur analyzed this activity in this way:

> I propose taking as the first philosophical use of recognition the pair identify/distinguish. To recognize something as the same, as identical to itself and not more than itself, implies distinguishing it from everything else. This first philosophical use [of recognition] verifies two semantic characteristics that we have seen connected to the use of the verb [to recognize] in the active voice – namely, the initiative of the mind in this mastery of meaning, and the initial quasi indistinguishableness of recognizing and knowing.[50]

This is one kind of knowing derived from one kind of recognition that comes to form my ideas about the seen order I conceive myself to inhabit, my location. But is it simply part of "my" seen order, only the knowledge seen by me? "That's your home!" my wife of over four decades exclaimed, who herself grew up a few blocks away, knowledge born of recognition from someone occupying a location, a concept of her seen order, that has more overlap with mine than other persons might have. And you, the reader, might travel to Richmond, Indiana, to the second house from the woods on Southwest 16th Street, take a picture on your cellphone and send to me to verify it exists in a seen order without my sight! And we might agree that

78   *Sighting the sacred unseen*

from your location when you were there and we weren't, and my wife and my location when we there and you weren't, the order we all three inhabit is the world with that object firmly known and recognized by us.

Immersion in a VRE involves the way human agency is "recognized" by the place-architecture. It is critical to the philosophical understanding of insider immersion as embodiment. The insiders' immersed residing as an embodying in one domain, the VRE, can affect life in the other domain, the ordinary outside. That it doesn't always simply reveals it is not a cause-and-effect relationship. But the nature of the exchange between place-architecture and insiders is a knowledge not within the domain shared by the scholar in the same way. To the active voice of the word "recognition," Ricouer adds an understanding of the word's passive voice, "I am recognized."[51] There is a different and additional knowledge exchange between place-architecture and VRE insider as the insider acts in a world structured as pliable to their agency, and it is a knowledge analogous to the classroom exchange between an instructor and the student who is called upon to respond to a question. Insides *are recognized* as part of giving the knowledgeable answer they held by active recognition. Within a sacred unseen order immersed insiders may display actions the scholar outside recognizes as neurological functions, social marginalization, or psychological condition. And knowing the nature of immersion and sense of presence in an order the interdisciplinary scholar understands as the new space of an overlapping domain, there is an additional knowledge. Insider sensation also involves the additional knowledge of being recognized; of being recognized while residing in a sacred unseen order, which the scholar is not. As in a VRE, the function of the activity for insiders in the domain of the sacred unseen order is they *are recognized* such that activity they are immersed in as bodies involves crossing a responsive place.

Imported from introduction for your evaluation

This import explains the sacred part, that the unseen order is sacred because insiders disclose "being recognized" for the insider human agency creates the order as something insiders know through recognition as part of the self and the social, integrated with the something more for insiders as "being recognized," a reciprocity simultaneously intimate and ultimate.

That yields another and deeper sense to recognition which in turn yields a different kind of knowledge because it does not involve our active recognizing, the identification by distinguishing from amongst objects and events. It is this kind of knowledge that is important to us in religious studies when we conceive of our aim as interpreting how activity functions for insiders. Insiders reside within these overlapping orders of the seen, shared with outsiders

Sighting the sacred unseen 79

like us, and the unseen, shared only with insiders. This insider unseen order contains some kind of extraordinary quality, extraordinary at least in that it is an element infused into the seen order and not, for the insider, generated exclusively by the seen. And this unseen order has an epistemological ramification for insiders that is not apparent to outsiders because they do not reside within it. Recognition can also be about being recognized; being seen; being known. Knowledge can also be the yield of "the dialectic of reflexivity and alterity through the figure of mutual recognition."[52] Every instructor encounters the situation where several students have raised their hands to answer a specific question and acknowledging a particular student from all those raised hands yields knowledge in addition to the verbally given correct fact. The student who is recognized knows themselves also to be known. In addition to all the ways insiders know themselves through the first sense of recognition, through this second sense, to be known, insiders have an addition to their identity denied to outsiders. This is part of the relationship between insiders and the unseen order generated by how their activity functions. Insider religious activity generates a sacred, unseen order. And residing there, they are known by it.

So, here again, knowledge as the yield of recognition is shaped by location. The first sense of knowledge from recognition is available both to insiders residing within religious activity and scholars studying insiders, who are outside of the insider activity but inside of the field of religious studies and the location of the university. The second sense of knowledge from recognition is part of insider residence within the sacred, unseen order generated by their activity, and scholars can at best use concepts scholars create to understand how activity functions religiously for insiders; that is, study how insider activity generates this sacred unseen order which, in residing within it, insiders are known by it and know themselves to be known in this way. Thus, it is through our concepts that we can understand the function of activity for insiders, and recognition of location and the knowledge produced through location that we can imagine insider's residence in that activity.

Circumscribing the seen in summary

If, as scholar David Tracy noted, analogy is similarity-in-difference, it's possible that studying how VREs function on insiders is a useful way to study human activity elsewhere. When you are inside of a VRE you are completely aware it is an order of time and space which your active responses shape, in ways like and unlike the world outside of the VRE. You reside in an order of time and space that is simultaneously like and unlike the world outside the VRE. Likewise, when you study individuals operating in a VRE,

80 *Sighting the sacred unseen*

it is obvious that they are in an order of time and space that you are not, an order that is unseen by you. And yet, you and they are inside of the ordinary world in that if the person in the VRE strays physically too far afield in the ordinary world, they might run into a desk or chair. As an observer you reside in the ordinary world of culture that includes the university, but the one in the VRE resides simultaneously in that ordinary world and a different one unseen to you. And in the case of persons with PTSD and higher functioning autism this simultaneity of overlapping orders – the sense of presence in a highly immersive virtual created world and returning to the ordinary order of time and space shared with you, the outside observer – generates an adaptation in the world outside the VRE, the ordinary world they share as a seen world with you and other outsiders.

When residing in a VRE the individual is in a generated space that can yield something transformative in the world outside that space. Yet, while residing there they are simultaneously still subject to the orders of time and space in the ordinary world outside of it. The function of the activity of residing inside a VRE is more deeply understood by employing concepts from religious studies. And the employment of those concepts – concepts derived from the integration of academia disciplinary yields – upon an activity outside the university, retools the concepts for subsequent use with activities of interest to the field.

How does the activity of residing inside a VRE function for insiders? The activity inside a VRE functions as a dynamic activity involving insider participatory construction of and residence in an unseen order of time and space that overlaps the seen, ordinary order shared with outsiders, those who are observing. This activity resembles the activity outsiders observe when studying insiders involved in the overlapping domain of the sacred-profane.

Thus, an interdisciplinary religious studies can retool the old concepts of the sacred and profane. During the 20th-century project to devise a science of religions, Mircea Eliade declared the sacred and profane as denoting "two modes of existence" that could be seen as "opposites." Shaped by 20th-century notions of universality, Eliade thought instances of the manifestation of the "sacred" exhibited characteristics no existing university discipline could discern, which became the reason for his participation in seeking to create a scientific discipline of the academic study of religions. The deconstructionist critiques of the social constructivism of that last three decades led scholars like McCutcheon and Arnal to conflate Eliade's opposites in their book title, *The Sacred Is the Profane*, liberating the academic study of religion from Enlightenment, scientific universality but with an equally deterministic cultural reductionism. Hints that what was being studied might contain something other than culture became viewed as a camouflaged theology. But, activity that might come into the purview of religious studies continues

Sighting the sacred unseen 81

outside the university, and any insistence that lived experience out there can be gathered and ordered as knowledge with conceptual packages produced in here disavows the dynamic relationship between scholar and insiders in the moment of engaged inquiry. When engaged with activity outside the university that could conceivably be understood more comprehensively through a complex and creative employment of the historical concepts of religious studies, integrated with findings from researchers in disciplines so as to be shaped for pragmatic use, moments of deep interpretation can unfold. The observer can interpret the function of insider activity in the creation of a space where the sacred, unseen order not shared with the outsider overlaps the seen, profane order that is shared. In insider activity generating this overlap, a space in-between the sacred and profane, or the sacred is the profane, is generated. And immersed in a new order of time and space with a sense of presence there – residing, in a word – this inextricable enfolding of mind with world inside an unseen order overlapping a seen one shared with outsiders, can function for the insider as a recognition. Or, something like the startled face of one of my students who, upon having spent a duration inside of a VRE, removed her goggles to exclaim, *Now I know what you mean when you say unseen order. And insider thoughts and movements in creating an overlapping space in-between. And being immersed and recognized.*

Notes

1 Cukor, Judith, et al., "Virtual Reality Exposure Therapy for Combat-Related PTSD," p. 73.
2 Paul Ricoeur, 2005, p. 19.
3 Ibid.
4 William James, 1961, p. 59.
5 Barbara O. Rothbaum, Larry F. Hodges, David Ready, Ken Graap, and Renato D. Alarcon, 2001. Retrieved at: www.psychiatrist.com/JCP/article/Pages/2001/v62n08/v62n0808.aspx
6 Judith Cukor, et al., "Virtual Reality Exposure Therapy for Combat-Related PTSD," *Posttraumatic Stress Disorder and Related Diseases in Combat Veterans*, E. C. Ritchie, editor, Springer International Publishing, Switzerland, 2015, p. 72.
7 Sarah Parsons and Peter Mitchell, "The Potential of Virtual Reality in Social Skills Training for People with Autistic Spectrum Disorders," *Journal of Intellectual Disability Research*, Vol. 46, No. 5 (June 2002), pp. 430–443. See especially Cukor, et al., 2015; Barbara O. Rothbaum, Larry F. Hodges, David Ready, Ken Graap, and Renato D. Alarcon, "Virtual Reality Exposure Therapy for Vietnam Veterans with Posttraumatic Stress Disorder, *Clinical Psychiatry*, (2001), Retrieved at: www.psychiatrist.com/JCP/article/Pages/2001/v62n08/v62n0808.aspx; and others.
8 James Welch, IV, 2011, p. 2.
9 William James, 1961, p. 59.
10 Wayne Proudfoot, January 2000, pp. 51–66.

82 *Sighting the sacred unseen*

11 Stephen Pattison, 2007, p. 39, note 35.
12 David Tracy, 2016, pp. 879–880.
13 Koji Komatsu, 2017, p. 16.
14 Ibid., p. 26.
15 Pattison, 2007, p. 45.
16 William James. Retrieved at: http://ebookcentral.proquest.com/lib/gvsu/detail.action?docID=563858
17 Eric Matthews, 2002, p. 8.
18 David Morris, 2004, p. 5.
19 Ibid.
20 Ibid., p. 6.
21 Ibid., p. 9.
22 Markus Gabriel, 2015, p. 7.
23 David E. Presti, 2018, p. 13.
24 Robert T. Tally, Jr., 2013, p. 41.
25 Dean Buonomano, 2017, pp. 77–78.
26 Marc Wittman, 2017, p. 10.
27 Ibid., p. 62.
28 Philip G. Zimbardo and John N. Boyd, 1999, pp. 1271–1272.
29 David Morris, 2018, p. 37.
30 James J. Cummings and Jeremy N. Bailenson, 2015, p. 3.
31 Anna Felnhofer, et al., 2015, pp. 48–56.
32 For more information and analysis see Stanford University's Virtual Human Interaction Lab and specifically the work of Jeremy N. Bailenson. Retrieved at: https://comm.stanford.edu/faculty-bailenson/
33 Felnhofer, et al., 2015.
34 Matthews, 2002, p. 8.
35 Rebekah J. Nelson, 2012, p. 172.
36 Felnhofer, et al., 2015, p. 54.
37 Carlo Rovelli, 2018, pp. 181–182.
38 Buonomano, 2017, p. 147.
39 Ibid., pp. 173, 178.
40 Juhani Pallasmaa, 2012, pp. 76, 67.
41 James, pp. 346, 349. Retrieved at: http://ebookcentral.proquest.com/lib/gvsu/detail.action?docID=563858
42 See Christelle Khadra, et al., 2018, pp. 343–353.
43 Kim Knott, 2005, p. 154 notes.
44 Morris, 2018, p. 5.
45 Ibid., p. 130.
46 Ibid., p. 157.
47 Ricoeur, 2005, p. 21.
48 Ibid., p. 25.
49 David Morgan, 2012, p. 185.
50 Ricoeur, 2005, p. 21.
51 Ibid., p. 248.
52 Ibid., p. 152.

4 Hierophany as an interdisciplinary concept

Because interdisciplinarity involves a scholar's self-consciousness in the most comprehensive manner possible, the scholar's personal context and cultural/historical location are understood to be a continuous part of knowledge production. This is especially present when scholars engage activity involving the insiders' construction of a sacred-profane unseen order in part because the manner of insider generation stirs the capacity of the scholar to circumscribe an order not seen nor inhabited. "No inquiry can be settled in a manner that is untouched by the interests of the inquirer"[1] and thus to be self-consciously interdisciplinary in religious studies means the scholar becomes familiar moving within the constant critique of personal architecture. Scholarly positionality never strays off of one's personal path. The scholar recognizes the unseen orders within which the "scholar as self" moves and at various times and locations, resides.

If location and the generation of new space are central traits of interdisciplinarity, then of course they should figure into interpretation. Location, though, is always fluid and thus evaluating how body movement functions is more complex than extracting objects to measure composition and effect or reducing it to activity from an "I." "In particular, the self is both something individual (just you or I) and something universal (each of us is a self) . . . [and] the discovery of the self takes place within the context of historical processes of self-knowledge."[2] It is constructed by analyzing human beings moving across the world and reflecting upon that "corporeal soil . . . not as insinuated into being by a reflective consciousness interrogating it from the outside, but as arising in the sinews and folds of a being that opens itself to question in a movement."[3]

And a new space in-between is generated by this kind of interdisciplinary self-consciousness, called a "third way" by Robert Orsi:

> between confessional or theological scholarship, on the one hand, and radically secular scholarship on the other . . . [that] is characterized by a disciplined suspension of the impulse to locate the other . . . securely

84 *Hierophany as an interdisciplinary concept*

in relation to one's own cosmos. It has no need to fortify the self in relation to the others; indeed, it is willing to make one's own self-conceptions vulnerable to the radically destabilizing possibilities of a genuine encounter with an unfamiliar way of life. This is an in-between orientation, located at the intersection of self and other, at the boundary between one's own moral universe and the moral world of the other. And it entails disciplining one's mind and heart to stay in this in-between place, in a posture of disciplined attentiveness, especially to difference.[4]

Going to class

I was trained in the academic study of religion and served as a parish minister before coming back into the university in 2010 to teach religious studies at a public university. I teach a class on "Religion and Love" where we use religious studies concepts to construct a lens to compare the function of insider activity in a variety of phenomena from a variety of locations. Recently we used an activity involving rings to describe and analyze the concept of the hierophany. I displayed my wedding ring, slid it off to display it, and asked who else had rings. One student showed what he called a "championship ring" and another what she called a "promise ring." I asked each to take the ring off, display it, and describe the actions that made up the phenomenon of receiving the particular rings, a kind of classroom "Trilogy of the Rings," as another student called it! In my experience students have to practice describing the activity that forms phenomena because they are so accustomed to substituting for description, the classifying and categorizing of activity, sometimes never actually describing. This is more than a casual observation in that students have been trained to extract activity out of its context as activity in order to deal with phenomena cognitively and reflectively.

I then added a fuller description of the activity involved in the phenomenon of receiving the wedding ring. It was part of a giving and receiving exchange, as these kinds of occasions often are. I was standing upon a raised platform in a church building we had been in only twice before, in front of a group of people half of whom I knew and half unknown to me, and looking at my companion and soulmate I adjusted my body stance and she adjusted hers in preparation, extended my left hand palm down as she gently took hold of it with one of her hands so as to use the other to slide round metal onto my third finger while repeating the phrase prompted by the minister. She looked at me in recognition and I looked at her while being recognized. Then, we both adjusted our bodies and she extended her hand as I slid the ring on her finger reciting words and looking upon her in my recognition of

Hierophany as an interdisciplinary concept 85

her as she was being recognized. As I was describing to the class I repeatedly slid my ring slowly from the knuckle to the tip of my finger to display the action as it was being described, a daily habitual action for me. I chimed in that I had performed close to a thousand wedding ceremonies during my 27 years in the parish ministry. I described the activity of one ceremony in particular, 20 years later in a different church building when I officiated at the wedding of a close friend's daughter who was four years older than our daughter. He had walked his daughter down the aisle of the church, and as was a custom, joined her hand with the hand of the person she would marry, leaving her as he sat in the front pew. I have been involved in the giving and receiving of a wedding ring as an insider – a first-order experience – to the time, place, and prescribed activities surrounding the giving and receiving as an officiant directing activity, and now as an outsider in a classroom studying phenomena involving giving and receiving rings as an insider moving in the location of the university. Being cognizant of positionality involves the recognition of the overlapping domains of outsider and insider, that as categories they do signify, but with fluid, and not rigid and absolute boundaries. Insider/outsider is, of course, a relative designation, but more than signifying objective or subjective location, the active performance, the body-action is central to what those designations often don't quite hold in their signification. Those locations are composed of activity, of how, when we occupy them, we *move about within where we are and during what time it is.* And in the classroom we as a class identified that in addition to discussing the activity involving phenomena regarding receiving and giving rings, we were also studying memory!

Our conversation on the concept of hierophany involved the history of the university as a location of knowledge production emphasized throughout the semester, the concepts of sacred and profane addressed in earlier weeks, seen and unseen orders of bounded time and space also addressed in earlier weeks, and hierophany. While sitting in a public university classroom, within the field of the academic study of religion, we considered in as much detail as we could the location we were currently occupying and the positionality of each of us in that location. The practice of determining personal location is a continuous part of scholarly self-consciousness and even bears the mark of a rite of passage of one from student to scholar. Yet, each of us composes personal location with different characteristics. All rings are round but there is little that is universal about their use when it comes to meaning. They are worn on fingers, toes, through noses, and involve no single event or series of events universally. Every occasion involving them has a particularity of location and occasion, culture and practice. In weddings I've performed there were a few occasions when the woman received a ring and the man didn't, and up until the last years in parish work in

86 *Hierophany as an interdisciplinary concept*

the exchanging of rings, same sex couples were witnessing an activity that held no legal standing for them, all variations of insider/outsider signification and corporeal motion, personal meaning and political and cultural significance. Wendy Doniger, who has compiled so many different narratives involving rings in the encyclopedic quest to chronicle as much of their varied uses as she can, pointed out that "some paleo-anthropologists regard this moment . . . around 70,000 years ago . . . when we started using personal ornamentation – rather than the moment when we first developed language or created painted images – as the moment when we became genuinely human."[5] Setting narratives side-by-side reveals resemblances even as probing for connections tempts paleo-anthropologists towards over-belief.

Yet, there is a space in-between claims of universal significance, the objective claim of a location without location, and confining claims to culture and individual meaning, the subjective claim of a world composed only of various locations; that is, between

> the contextualist position . . . an extrapolation of Kantian epistemology [that] experience is always influenced and constrained by prior experience, learning, and language . . . [and] essentialism . . . [which] holds that while the contextualist thesis may describe the vast majority of experience, there is a certain subset of experiences – rare, but significant nonetheless – that partake of a different structure altogether.[6]

Ring giving and receiving is neither rare nor confined and constrained by prior experience. There is the sensation of a substance, in this case metal, being placed upon your finger by another who is holding your hand and uttering sounds that like all spoken words will fade in time; there is the readjustment of bodies before repeating the activity when the other extends and you gently grab hold, guiding the ring onto the finger of another, bodies moving across the earth and through the air; performed in a location and time that is not repeatable but is somehow related to the memory of it that is generated in the feeling of gliding the ring from the knuckle to the fingertip.

The first instance involves residing in an overlapping domain, "not outside that which is expressed yet is nonetheless distinct from that which is expressed,"[7] while the second is the remembrance of residing in that overlapping domain, which itself is residing in an overlapping domain! And the remembrance that was involved in the classroom discussion? Still another, a complexity which the philosopher identifies as the "problem posed by the entanglement of memory and imagination . . . [in posing the memory as] the present representation of an absent thing . . . enclosing the problematic of memory within that of imagination."[8] And which the neurologist poses

Hierophany as an interdisciplinary concept   87

from a different location as "a fundamental problem . . . [in that] the flow of time is . . . a mental construct, but of something that holds no equivalent in the physical world."[9] So every semester when our unit on hierophany occurs and we engage in this story, familiar for the professor but new for the students; involving the professor and his metal band and his finger *and the sliding* and the student's sensation of seeing, then reflecting; the professor residing in a string of memories from an initiating event to an event in the future where the physical companionship will be no more alongside the students residing only in the event in its present iteration both the professor and the students are involved in recognition as knowledge of the linguistic meaning of hierophany and the arguments of essentialists and social constructionists, while the professor being recognized is an additional imaginative engagement that involves the presence of his companion who is absent in the room because she is working across campus! There are a complexity of overlapping domains but different ones involving time and place, seeing and touching, recognition and being recognized.

In other words, there are at work relationships of bodies to places and times, different forms of knowledge through different forms of recognition, and different qualities of time and place as being felt. Place functions in these moments in the church where I gave and received recognition, a different church and city 20 years later officiating at my friend's daughter's wedding, and the description in the classroom this semester. There the object in relationship to space and the movement of bodies through those spaces that were part of each phenomenon and phenomena. There is time on several levels, the sequence of events from my wedding, my friend's daughter's 20 years later, and my classroom retelling 20 more years later. But it is the phenomenon of giving and receiving rings with my companion that holds a quality involving time that unlike other memories of other past rings moments feels present. And there is one continuous object, the ring, continuous through sensations in various places at different times, the sliding on and off as is my habitual motion that simultaneously feels present by the insider, me. And there is the Self in its widest conception, how our connection to others forms part of our identity, our sense of being an autonomous and whole Self, a "presence in absence"[10] involving my wife working on the other side of campus. How does that sensation of that object moving across my finger function religiously?

A wide variety of disciplinary yields might help us, from history, culture, sociology, anthropology, and more, using critical, post-colonial, decolonial methodologies. But, we are looking for particular disciplinary yields to perform an interdisciplinary, hermeneutical interpretation using embodied phenomenology in part because that is the location that integrates the interpreter's academic location with locations from his previous professional and personal

88   *Hierophany as an interdisciplinary concept*

life, and in part because that will allow us to use productively the concepts we've previously retooled – the sacred-profane as a new space, an overlapping domain of the seen and unseen order of structured time and place. Here again, interdisciplinarity's historical perspective as a parallax view, in the case here of the epistemological history of the university, an approach that moves beyond "articulating and applying the right epistemological theory or experiential model . . . [and towards] an effective interpretive method that reveals the understanding of experience that is already embedded within specific experiential accounts."[11] The giving and receiving of the ring functions as a corporeal hierophany in the manifestation of a new space for knowledge production, the overlapping domain of the sacred-profane unseen order within which the insider resides through performing a sacred gaze.

Eliade identified the hierophany as "*the act of manifestation* of the sacred,"[12] which was as we've noted above part of the creation of a universal object for scientific study. It cannot designate that here for the world does not exist as seen from a location that is no location, from objectivity with no spectators. Nor will the hierophany designate something that is exclusively confined to cultural production. It also cannot designate that for the world does not exist as only location, from subjectivity only with spectators. Our push is for something other than the space created by the contest between these two, another contender emerging from the intentional creation of a new space for knowledge production. The hierophany will designate an event occurring as insiders reside corporeally in the overlapping domain of the sacred-profane. The generation of the overlapping domain and the residence there are what this interdisciplinary religious studies scholar will study in a manner consistent with personal and professional location, that is, a particular positionality.

This overlapping domain is structured by the integration of time and place in order to generate the sensations of residence in that domain. The impression of space upon persons in humanly created physical structures emulate the other prominent place of residence, nature:

> A walk through a forest is invigorating and healing due to the constant interaction of all sense modalities . . . The eye collaborates with the body and the other senses. One's sense of reality is strengthened and articulated by this contact interaction. Architecture is essentially an extension of nature into the man-made realm, providing the ground for perception and the horizon of experiencing and understanding the world. It is not an isolated and self-sufficient artefact; it directs our attention and existential experience to wider horizons.[13]

Architecture involves not only space arranged to press upon human beings to generate sensation of a particular sort, but the assumption "that everyone

Hierophany as an interdisciplinary concept 89

receives information about the environment *through his or her senses*"[14] and not just through the visual sense. And, finally, that this is before cognition and reflection.

And, yet, mental activity is involved after the sensory impression of receiving and giving the ring in the initial encounter, and definitely becomes part of the activity in the classroom of recalling it 40-plus years after the event. While the nature of mental activity in the latter case is contested one position might argue that it "involve[s] thought and reason that target distal, absent, highly abstract, or even impossible state of affairs."[15] Mental activity of the most conceptually complex nature occurs as thinking is disengaged and taken out of the context of the original phenomenon. However, some have reconsidered, as when "concreate external symbols . . . create conditions of (what I shall call) surrogate situatedness . . . [whereby] we reason about what is not at hand by means of dense looping interactions with a variety of stable external structures that stand in for absent states of affairs."[16]

The wedding ring sliding from the knuckle to the tip of the finger and back down, simultaneously stands in for what is absent, the moment, and is the moment felt. The integrative action and object generate a surrogate situatedness that simultaneously overlaps the situatedness of the initial location in the two forms of recognition held by the action with the object.

This overlapping domain of situatedness and surrogate situatedness is also structured by a confluence of time as experienced ordinarily and through constructive activity, time as experienced extraordinarily, but in a specific way that is instigated by the sensation of constructed space and integrated with that. The present to the wedded insider contains both presentist time as sequentially constructed by the brain and "felt" (past-present-future) and shared with the student observers, and eternalist time as a confluence of past and future with the present. I am here in this particular space and time with my students while simultaneously occupying a time and place where there is nothing of that the mind would designate as time, and space; no sequence, and no special powers to this space (the classroom) or that space (the church). To some it is the disciplinary contest between the neurologists and the physicists. To the interdisciplinary religious studies scholar it is the complexities involved in residing in an overlapping domain characterized by simultaneity. And, as was pointed out earlier, this integration of time and place, generating sensations of residence in an overlapping domain structured by time and space felt as a simultaneity, generates a sacred-profane unseen order that functions to produce two kinds of knowledge to insiders; recognizing the ring as the one given to me in a corporeal exchange whereby I was recognized.

David Morgan helps to identify how the sensation of sight functions in complimenting the skin's touching the metal ring in its undulation. The sacred gaze instigates and is involved in a "way of seeing . . . [that] exerts the power to arrest the mind and deliver if from the anxieties that fragment

90   *Hierophany as an interdisciplinary concept*

consciousness and bind it to such invented torments as frustration, rage, jealousy, or obsession,"[17] to which I would add not only deliver it from but also into anxieties that fragment. There is power involved in some exchanges between seer and seen.

The nature of power in this ocular, sensate exchange is graspable if not apparent to outsider observers. Given this context it is a manifestation of power of being recognized when involved in a gaze as more than a glance, not narrow like a stare, but looking with self-conscious intent at an object set apart from other objects, in a visual exchange transformed into a particular kind of knowledge:

> . . . knowing does not seem exclusively to involve the evidence of sight, since any visual activity on the part of the viewer would have the same effect. Indeed, in addition to the evidence of the ocular senses, one also needs to be able to recognize the difference between sensing, feeling – noticing that the sensorium has been stimulated – and knowing. In other words, one has to be able to recognize what it might *feel* like to be knowing something, to feel the interleaving of the affective with the cognitive . . . to witness that I am looking before I can begin to see this image; in this sense looking is not like a visual activity at all – it is more like a recognition of presences, or a feeling of or for presence . . . my own identification of self-presence.[18]

To be recognized. It is this form of knowledge that is eternalist and the continuously-sequential-presentist simultaneously. Insider residence involves a certain feeling of the integration of time and place and persons such that the generated domain is felt bodily as a returning recognition. The heightened quality is part of domain residence. While performing the activity of exchanging rings couples will laugh hysterically, cry uncontrollably, smile intoxicatingly, and in the foyer afterward confess their utter dislocation and disorientation while they are showing one another the rings on their fingers. Or not. Not everybody does this, nor needs to in order to elicit interest. It's neither a universal response let along a universal custom, and sometimes the change in personal identity and social location aren't felt. But that it occurs in multiple occasions in multiple locations, even in different cultures, is evidence that residing has occurred in a domain other than exclusively a particularist one especially in that recorded by cognition or not, the body will find itself moving within newly formed personal and social spaces with a newfound identity or status. The overlapping sacred-profane unseen order that insiders resided in not only are liminal locations but more.

Thus, in considering the retooled concept of the hierophany one can see that it involves corporeal residence in an overlapping domain wherein

Hierophany as an interdisciplinary concept 91

objects are what they are simultaneously to something more. They now hold that overlapping domain especially to the extent the object interacts with the bodies and the movement of bodies of insiders. But there is an effect on the state of consciousness of insiders for which James notes in the extreme case of the mystical experience and which can be extrapolated on a spectrum of phenomena to include my ring exchange:

> Mystical states [of consciousness] cannot be sustained for long . . . often, when faded, their quality can but imperfectly be reproduced in memory, but when they recur it is recognized; and from one recurrence to another it is susceptible of continuous development in what is felt as inner richness and importance.[19]

This would suggest the prospect of my habit today with my ring and finger deepens my sense of being recognized regardless of whether my wife is even present in the room.

Returning to the scholar's study

Thus, while standing in the classroom or sitting in the scholar's study and performing the knowledge-gathering process, when scholars are involved in the identification of an object of study and the creation of concepts and methods in a particular way so as to study that object, they are performing knowledge production in a particular way. This is a disciplinary approach defined as "sets of problems, methods, and research practices or as bodies of knowledge . . . [and] social [and professional] networks of individuals interested in related problems or ideas."[20] Regardless of whether we call ourselves a discipline or field at meetings of the American Academy of Religion our ground location is the Western university where disciplines appeared as products of the late 19th early 20th centuries, a result and accelerant of increased specialization in knowledge gathering; that is, in breeding knowledge silos. We might argue "field" or "discipline" in a location where that is understood as having different characteristics and value. Regardless of designation, though, the disciplinary knowledge-gathering processes can be exercised in locations distant from where the activity occurs in its "location." And this distance distorts. A human cell lifted out of the body, placed between two microscopic plates, and observed under a microscope is not the cell in the body. Concepts and methodologies are critiqued in the scholar's study to be refined before applying them to activities outside the location where they were formed. Building a car from the design room to the production line is different than driving it on the road.

92 *Hierophany as an interdisciplinary concept*

Various disciplines do not exist independently of one another but on a campus, a physical or virtual location where the epistemological project also orders the knowledge gathered into a unity that is understandable, the *universitas* whose physical symbol is the library. Knowledge ordering has a history that directs knowledge gathering. For our purposes here it is enough to say that as an epistemological project the university was given birth by the intellectual organizing principles of European, white, male, medieval Christian *theology* to which philosophy and science were servants. As understood then, "Faith precedes science, fixes its boundaries, and prescribes it conditions."[21] Enlightenment philosophy later usurped Christian theology as the university's intellectual organizing principle, with theology and science as its servants. J. Z. Smith noted this turn in telling of David Hume's part in constructing natural religion. The Protestant Reformation, as designating the events breaking up Christianity's institutional homogeneity and theological unification, assisted in this turn away from theology and towards philosophy's reconceiving in the concept of "natural religion," aided by the European colonialist expansion into cultures unlike itself. And for the past two centuries modern, empirical science has gradually taken the reins of command of the university's epistemological organizing principle over philosophy and what had become natural religion's concept of "religion." According to Whitehead science has done to knowledge organization and production what religion would do and has done by beginning with experience which moves to formulation. It's just that science is more camouflaged in its approach: "science can leave its metaphysics implicit and retire behind our belief in the pragmatic value of its general orientation . . . rest[ing, as it does] upon a naïve faith."[22] Still, like its rival, religion, science generates a metaphysics that consumes philosophy and its rival religion. This coronation of science as rule of the university epistemological realm is evident in the 20th century project to produce a "science of religions" with a universal object of study, the sacred, that could not be reduced to what existing disciplines could discern, and the early-21st-century declaration that this project was bankrupt. And now, the concerns raised about the viability of religious studies as a field, what to do with the concept of "religion," whether religious studies is a subfield of a social science and mired in what Robert Orsi has identified as the "hypostatization of method":

> If method is not fetishized into what you might find in a how-to manual, but if instead method has to do with the pragmatics of our work, it may broaden out to raise questions about what we do and how we live as scholars today, in the world as it is. Otherwise, what is so bad about foundering around?[23]

Hierophany as an interdisciplinary concept   93

What is wrong with every question being open especially as through a critique of the university as an epistemological project?

In other words, there is a relationship between location in this epistemological project, historically considered, and the anxiety over foundering around. The disciplinary knowledge-silos science requires privileges not only STEM – encouraged in the public university by the funding apparatus of state legislatures and the yearly guestimate as to where jobs will originate next – but also what Habermas labeled as "scientism," and the hand-wringing of a field struggling with direction and survival in an inhospitable location. The trajectory of knowledge-silos targets reductionism.

In his foundational book *Interdisciplinarity*, Joe Moran traced its transformative approach to the gathering and ordering of knowledge: "In this sense, interdisciplinarity interlocks with the concerns of epistemology . . . and tends to be centred around problems and issues that cannot be addressed or solved within the existing disciplines, rather than the quest for an all-inclusive synthesis."[24] Interdisciplinarity generates spaces in-between the disciplines and changes concepts forged in the academic study of religion's conceptual assertions in the 20th century and critique in the early 21st century. It disdains reductionism more than lines of inquiry, as distorting the complexity in activity beyond the university, beyond the university's epistemological organizing principles and current privileging, and beyond the hypostatizing concept and method. The concepts forged in the scholar's study must be fluid and imprecise enough to be shaped by the activity studied outside the university. And, when the scholar returns to the study and into the classroom the demand will be to integrate the concept as reshaped by experience with disciplinary yields in the university location, to generate a new and more comprehensive understanding, incomplete and imprecise as it will be. Interdisciplinary integration generates novelty. Jason Blum's view of William James, the consummate interdisciplinarian, hints at what this involves: "James's view of experience boldly revises – or, more accurately, rejects – Western epistemology in favor of a perspective that emphasizes the vague, affective, dynamic, and ineffable dimensions of experience in addition to its lucid, discursive, logical aspects."[25] James' drive was "getting behind epistemology in order to examine the nature and function of experience itself."[26]

James' style of performing methodology was to integrate not only the concepts as dealt with by various disciplines in the university lecture halls, but in doing so he also recognized how the scholar was transformed by engaging activity outside the university and before critical reexamination. Certain activities impress upon participants in the overlapping domains of insider and outsider status, and for us, the sacred/profane. The metallic ring bought at Sears holds both that discounted price and something more

94 *Hierophany as an interdisciplinary concept*

generated when it is placed upon the ring by a beloved to a beloved. Experience involves the embodiment of a certain finger extended, the sensation of the hand held by another with a circled metallic hardness sliding upon the skin's surface, and the thinking necessary to repeat words and make promises. And when it is recalled over 40 years later it carries with it a history of what cannot totally be circumscribed by concept nor examined by memory studies alone. David Morgan describes Material Religion as studying "the way in which an object participates in making and sustaining a life-world."[27] And how residing in the various overlapping domains form world orders for insiders.

Notes

1 Wayne Proudfoot, "William James on an Unseen Order," *The Harvard Theological Review*, Vol. 93, No. 1 (January 2000), pp. 51–66, 53.
2 Markus Gabriel, 2017, p. 176.
3 David Morris, 2004, p. 82.
4 Robert Orsi, 2005, p. 198.
5 Wendy Doniger, *The Ring of Truth and Other Myths of Sex and Jewelry*, Oxford University Press, New York, 2017. Print, p. 1.
6 Jason Blum, 2015, p. 2.
7 Morris, 2004.
8 Paul Ricoeur, 2000, p. 7.
9 Dean Buonomano, 2017, p. 216.
10 William James, 1900, p. 44.
11 Blum, 2015, p. 4.
12 Mircea Eliade, 1996, p. 11.
13 Juhani Pallasmaa, 2012, pp. 44–45.
14 Edward T. Hall, 1966, p. xi.
15 Andy Clark, 2005, pp. 233–234.
16 Ibid.
17 David Morgan, 2005, p. 1.
18 Peter De Bolla, *Art Matters*, Harvard University Press, Cambridge, 2003. Print. pp. 48–49.
19 William James, 1961, p. 300.
20 Lisa R. Lattuca, *Creating Interdisciplinarity*, Vanderbilt University Press, Nashville, 2001. Print, p. 23.
21 Charles Homer Haskins, 1923, p. 71, quoting Alzog, *Church History* (1876), II, p. 733.
22 Alfred North Whitehead, 1926, p. 83.
23 Robert Orsi, 2016, p. 264.
24 Joe Moran, *Interdisciplinarity*, Routledge, New York, 2002, p. 15.
25 Blum, 2015, p. 424.
26 Ibid., p. 426.
27 Morgan, 2017, p. 15.

5 A summary and summons

We have sought to understand more fully what is meant when a religious studies scholar describes our study as "interdisciplinary." Interdisciplinarity has here been named as a style of performing methodology whose trajectory is towards the establishment of a space in-between the university-generated disciplinary structures, a new location for the production of knowledge. Within this new space interdisciplinary knowledge is generated through an integration of disciplinary yields.

Fundamental to interdisciplinarity is the construction of a deep, comprehensive self-consciousness regarding location. For the religious studies scholar this requires a unique understanding of personal location in relationship to professional location. The intertwining cultural reality of the practice of religion with the study of religion yields a positionality towards scholarly work that requires the integration of personal history into scholarly work, analogous in part to autoethnography, or, at the very least, some form of accounting for the relationship between scholar and subject. Because of this natural characteristic of the relationship between scholar and subject in religious studies, interdisciplinarity performance in this location is distinctive from disciplinary work. While the anthropologist is part of a culture, a sociologist belongs to some group, a psychologist has a psyche, and a philosopher has thoughts, it is the religious studies scholar who must account for personal location to subject in a distinctive way. It is not unusual for the scholar to be questioned by students, "What do you believe?" or "Are you an atheist?" or to be asked at a faculty meeting with other academics considering whether to approve of the creation of a religious studies major, "How can religion be taught in the public university?" or "Will you have a Muslim teach Islam, a Christian Christianity, etc.?" These complex questions involving location are unique to the field and thus, the interdisciplinary religious studies scholar must perform a critique of personal location knowing that personal location influences scholarly positionality in ways peculiar to the field.

96 *A summary and summons*

In addition, interdisciplinarity requires the scholar to develop a self-conscious, intentional critique of the professional location as integral to interdisciplinary knowledge formation. Here a particular critique has been offered of the university as an epistemological project. It is not meant to be comprehensive as it is apparent so much has been left out: colonialism and empire, or gender, or race, or funding, technology, public and private forms of education, student population demographic changes, and a myriad of other variables, all of which have shaped and are still shaping universities. The history presented here has been a philosophical history of knowledge production in the university because from this author's point of view, reconsidering that epistemological history assists religious studies in the midst of the complex identity issues it is facing. While the university is a historical institution in the culture of the West, has been part and parcel of politically driven agendas out of Europe from the medieval era through the United States unto our own time, this book has chosen a kind of critique whereby interdisciplinarity's aim – to create a space in-between disciplines for new knowledge production – can help locate religious studies in the university.

In the West, the university's knowledge production is driven by epistemic organizing principles that shape what is deemed worthy to be gathered as the raw materials of knowledge, and how it is delivered out to the world. Since the beginning of the university in the West three knowledge domains have contended for prominence in any given era in history: philosophy, science, and religion, with dramatic changes in each era as to what constituted a general understanding as to what was being studied as religion. At the founding of the university it was the epistemological organizing principles of medieval Christian theology that governed over philosophy and science and which knitted the knowledge produced by the university into a unitary "body of knowledge." Augustinian understandings of how knowledge revealed an ultimate Christian purpose to existence were prominent as a transition was occurring as to where educational preparation for the "religious life" occurred, from the monastery to the cathedral university. Philosophy was performed in service to Christian theology, the era's scholasticism, and science developed as a means to analyze the natural world as an of embodiment divine purpose.

The organizing principles of the university began to change as Christianity itself changed during the Reformation through the Enlightenment. The Reformation changed where the religious life was led, from the monastery and cathedral out into the city and its population, and the changes in how the university produced knowledge reflected this. The fracturing of Christianity dissolved the unity that the medieval age had brought to society and around which the university had been organized fully and completely,

A summary and summons 97

and two "books" emerged for which education prepared one to "read": the Book of Scripture and the Book of Nature. As the Christian Scriptures emerged as the sole authority in the reforming spirit that took hold in Christianity, the locus of authority shifted from the dissolved Christendom to the authority of individual interpretation grounded in Scripture. Education was critical not only for the populace to read the Scriptures but to interpret it accurately as well. And nature was "read" too, like a book, and interest developed in understanding the natural world as its own form of divine revelation. God's purposes could be studied and rendered in the movement of the planets and in the nature's laws as surely, and in some cases even more readily than in the arcane machinations of Church bureaucracy and papal pronouncement.

This continued until the Enlightenment coalesced intellectual forces to make the transition complete in the university as an epistemological project. It was the result of the confluence of so many factors as is the case with anything that emerges in history, but the results were unmistakably evident. Philosophy surpassed Christianity as forming the organizing principles around which university produced knowledge became a unitary, body of knowledge. This age of the great philosophers changed how both science and religion were understood. Modern empirical science emerged, and religion came to be studied and understood through a division of it into theology and natural religion. Gradually each developed in contest with the other growing distinctively in methodologies and aims.

The modern era saw the fullest effect of the Enlightenment science in the 19th century's increased specialization of natural science and in the generation of the social sciences. This has continued to our day with unparalleled advancements in for example, medical science, the health sciences, engineering, and in technological advancements that today surpass yesterday at breakneck speed. Institutional changes in the university embody this. The disciplinary structure has yielded the complexities of increased specialization with its burgeoning storehouse of newly gathered knowledge, the creation of new disciplines unheard of when philosophy and Christendom systematized the university's epistemic aims, and the appearance of a "siloed" quality in how the *universitas* goes about doing what it does. Research universities arose with funding by state support and the privileging of STEM, and the creation and rise of computer science. Libraries are no longer the centralized location for organizing and disseminating knowledge as student laptops and cell phones give them access to texts and other resources from around the world.

But there has been an "epistemological cost" to this over-production brought about by the organizing principles of the modern university. Like religion did with science and philosophy in the earliest stages of

98   *A summary and summons*

the university, science tends towards a dominating metaphysics; hence, the rise of the philosophy of science and the 20th-century pursuit to generate a science of religions. Increasingly, specialization in disciplinary tasks has also borne a certain disconnected quality to knowledge formation and an attendant distance between what is done in the scholar's study and the university lab. The capacity of university produced knowledge to address problems rising in the world that cannot fit neatly into scientifically generated disciplinary formats. It is this breach that gave rise to interdisciplinarity.

Interdisciplinarity is a style of performing methodology that is neither akin to nor in opposition to disciplinary knowledge formation. It is a different addition, a "something other." It integrates the yields of disciplinary specialization internal to the university, through scholarly engagement with phenomena outside the university, fulfilling the expressed aim and intention to create a new space for knowledge than what specialization and internal university processes can generate alone. If accumulating knowledge can transform the student, then interdisciplinarity represents that the knowledge-making process can itself be transformative in its performance.

Understanding interdisciplinarity so as to perform methodologies in this style gives religious studies scholarship more intentionality and a deeper self-consciousness to its scholars. When a scholar performs a historical analysis of concepts, tracing their history as a prelude to using them in performing a methodology, it foreshadows interdisciplinary work. But that alone does not make it interdisciplinary. If that history is used primarily or exclusively to evaluate and improve the academic study of religion, for example, then the location of the concepts' actual use is the university and its internal processes, and this reaffirms how the university produces knowledge through which it may deepen understanding. That is not interdisciplinarity but a confirmation that the way knowledge is produced as practiced and structured in the modern university needs no adjustment when performing study, no "something other." However, if the conceptual history is told with the self-conscious intent of using that history to retool the concept as the scholar evaluates how activity functions in phenomena outside the university, then interdisciplinarity is in play. And finally, if the aims of performing the historicizing of concepts and bringing them outside the university to engage phenomena is aimed towards generating a space in-between what disciplinarity and speciality hold, then interdisciplinarity is fully engaged. The epistemological tilt of interdisciplinarity is away from using reductionisms to close inquiry – recalling Whitehead's admonishment to science, "seek simplicity and distrust it"[1] – and into a deeper recognition of the distinction between the concept as devised inside the university, and phenomenal sensate complexity, and that maintaining this distinction becomes the scholar's best defense against what William James called vicious intellectualism:

> The treating of a name as excluding from the fact named what the name's definition fails positively to include . . . A good illustration of this is to be found in a controversy between Mr. Bradley and the present writer . . . Mr. Bradley contending . . . that "resemblance" is an illegitimate category, because it admits of degrees, and that the only real relations in comparison are absolute identity and absolute non-comparability.[2]

There are interdisciplinary performances of methodology populating much of the exciting new research arising the last few decades and these bear the style's characteristics. For example, the space in-between is called a "third way" by Robert Orsi:

> between confessional or theological scholarship, on the one hand, and radically secular scholarship on the other . . . [that] is characterized by a disciplined suspension of the impulse to locate the other . . . securely in relation to one's own cosmos. It has no need to fortify the self in relation to the others; indeed, it is willing to make one's own self-conceptions vulnerable to the radically destabilizing possibilities of a genuine encounter with an unfamiliar way of life. This is an in-between orientation, located at the intersection of self and other, at the boundary between one's own moral universe and the moral world of the other. And it entails disciplining one's mind and heart to stay in this in-between place, in a posture of disciplined attentiveness, especially to difference.[3]

The 20th century claims of a concept's universal quality and the 21st century's critique of it as particular, as is the case with the sacred and profane, reveal the complicity of scientific organizing principles in the modern university. They influenced how a science of religions needed to be constructed with a universal phenomenon at its core, and how that pursuit needed to be abandoned when that core was critiqued as ill conceived. They shape the uncertainties of a field of research where the personal history of the scholar – the scholar's subjectivity – is implicated in the impossibilities of treating the phenomena studied in a scientifically objective manner. And today there remain deep concerns about the viability of religious studies as

100 *A summary and summons*

a field, what to do with the concept of "religion," and what Robert Orsi has identified as the "hypostatization of method."

> If method is not fetishized into what you might find in a how-to manual, but if instead method has to do with the pragmatics of our work, it may broaden out to raise questions about what we do and how we live as scholars today, in the world as it is. Otherwise, what is so bad about foundering around?[4]

What is wrong indeed?, except that no self-respecting discipline would be caught "foundering around"!

In other words, there is a relationship between location in this epistemological project historically considered and the anxiety over foundering around. The disciplinary knowledge-silos science requires privileges not only STEM – encouraged in the public university by the funding apparatus of state legislatures and their yearly habit of guessing where jobs in the future will originate – but also what Habermas labeled as "scientism," and the hand-wringing of a field struggling with direction.

Through an interdisciplinary lens formed by an epistemological critique of the university location and religious studies' place in it, there is something other, much more other than seeing the field through the lens of the disciplines of social science or philosophy or theology alone. And this has been the purpose of this book and the intent of the author. To explain and perform interdisciplinarity.

Notes

1 Alfred North Whitehead, 1919, p. 208.
2 William James, 1977, pp. 32, 36n.
3 Robert Orsi, 2005, p. 198.
4 Robert Orsi, 2016, p. 264.

Bibliography

Aoun, Joseph E., *Robot-Proof: Higher Education in the Age of Artificial Intelligence*, The MIT Press, Cambridge, MA, 2017, p. 142, quoting Vannevar Bush, *Science: The Endless Frontier*, United States Government Printing Office, Washington, DC, 1945. Retrieved at: https://nsf.gov/about/history/vbush1945.htm

Arnal, William and McCutcheon, Russell, *The Sacred Is the Profane: The Political Nature of "Religion,"* Oxford University Press, Oxford, 2012. Print.

Bainton, Roland H., *Early and Medieval Christianity*, Beacon Press, Boston, 1962. Print.

Blum, Jason N., "William James on How to Study Experience: Integrating Phenomenology of Religion and Radical Empiricism," *Method and Theory in the Study of Religion*, Vol. 27 (2015), pp. 423–446.

―――, *Zen and the Unspeakable God*, The Pennsylvania State University Press, University Park, PA, 2015. Print.

Buonomano, Dean, *Your Brain Is a Time Machine: The Neuroscience and Physics of Time*, W.W. Norton and Company, New York, 2017. Print.

Chadwick, Henry, *Augustine of Hippo: A Life*, Oxford University Press, New York, 2009. Print.

Chang, Heewon, *Autoethnography as Method*, Left Coast Press, Inc., Walnut Creek, CA, 2008, pp. 48–49 as quoted in *Critical Autoethnography*, Boylorn and Orbe, editors, 2014. Print.

Clark, Andy, "Beyond the Flesh: Some Lessons from a Mole Cricket," *Artificial Life*, Vol. 11 (2005), pp. 233–244.

"Condemnation of Errors at Paris in 1241," D.C. Munro, Translations and Reprints (Philadelphia: University of Pennsylvania Press), Vol II, No. 3, as quoted in *The Medieval World: 300–1300*, Norman F. Cantor, ed., Macmillan Publishing Company, Inc., 1968. Print.

Cukor, Judith, et al., "Virtual Reality Exposure Therapy for Combat-Related PTSD," *Posttraumatic Stress Disorder and Related Diseases in Combat Veterans*, E. C. Ritchie, editor, Springer International Publishing, Switzerland, 2015.

Cummings, James J. and Bailenson, Jeremy N., "How Immersive Is Enough? A Meta-Analysis of the Effect of Immersive Technology on User Presence," *Media Psychology*, Routledge, 2015. Retrieved at: http://vhil.stanford.edu/mm/2015/cummings-mp-how-immersive.pdf

102   Bibliography

De Bolla, Peter, *Art Matters*, Harvard University Press, Cambridge, 2003. Print.

Deleuze, Gilles and Guattari, Felix, *What Is Philosophy?*, Columbia University Press, New York, 1994. Print.

de Vries, Hent, "Introduction: Why Still 'Religion'?," *Religion: Beyond a Concept*, Hent de Vries, editor, Fordham University Press, New York, 2008. Print.

Dimock, Edward C., Jr., "Līlā," *History of Religions*, Vol. 29, No. 2 (November 1989).

Doniger, Wendy, *The Ring of Truth and Other Myths of Sex and Jewelry*, Oxford University Press, New York, 2017. Print.

Durkheim, Emile, *The Elementary Forms of Religious Life*, Hollen Street Press, Ltd, London, 1915. Print.

Eliade, Micrea, *The Sacred and the Profane*, Harper and Row Publishers, New York, 1957. Print.

————, *Patterns in Comparative Religion*, Rosemary Sheed, trans., University of Nebraska Press, Lincoln, NE, 1958. Print.

Engelstad, Ericka and Gerrard, Siri, "Introduction," *Challenging Situatedness: Gender, Culture and the Production of Knowledge*, Ericka Engelstad and Siri Gerrard, editors, Eburon Academic Publishers, The Netherlands, 2005. Print.

Felnhofer, Anna, et al., "Is Virtual Reality Emotionally Arousing? Investigating Five Emotion Inducing Virtual Park Scenarios," *International Journal of Human-Computer Studies*, Vol. 82 (2015). Retrieved at: www.journals.elsevier.com/international-journal-of-human-computer-studies

Ferruolo, Stephen C., *The Origins of the University: The Schools of Paris and Their Critics, 1100–1215*, Stanford University Press, Stanford, 1985. Print.

Fong, Benjamin Y., "On Critics and What's Real: Russell McCutcheon on Religious Experience," *Journal of the American Academy of Religion*, Vol. 82, No. 4 (December 2014).

Fuller, Steve, "Chapter Four: Deviant Interdisciplinarity," *The Oxford Handbook of Interdisciplinarity*, Robert Frodeman, editor, Oxford University Press, New York, 2010. Print.

Gabriel, Markus, *Why the World Does Not Exist*, Gregory S. Moss, trans., Polity Press, Cambridge, UK, 2015. Print.

————, *I Am Not a Brain: Philosophy of Mind for the Twenty-First Century*, Christopher Turner, trans., Polity Press, Berlin, 2017. Print.

Gillespie, Ryan, "Reason, Religion, and Postsecular Liberal-Democratic Epistemology," *Philosophy and Rhetoric*, Vol. 47, No. 1 (2014), Penn State University Press.

Gorski, Philip and Altinordu, Ates, "After Secularization," *Annual Review of Sociology*, Vol. 34 (2008), pp. 55–85, 60.

Habermas, Jurgen, *Knowledge and Human Interests*, Jeremy J. Shapiro, trans., Beacon Press, Boston, 1971. Print.

Hall, Edward T., *The Hidden Dimension*, Random House, Inc., New York, 1966. Print.

Haskins, Charles Homer, *The Rise of Universities*, Henry Holt and Company, New York, 1923. Print.

James, William, *The Meaning of Truth*, Longmans Breen and Company, New York, 1900. Print.

————, *The Principles of Psychology*, Volume One, Dover Publications, Inc., New York, 1950 edition. Print.

Bibliography   103

———, *The Varieties of Religious Experience: A Study in Human Nature*, Collier Books, New York, 1961. Print.

———, *A Pluralistic Universe*, Harvard University Press, Cambridge and London, 1977. Print.

———, "Reflex Action and Theism," *The Will to Believe and Other Essays in Popular Philosophy*, The Floating Press, 2010, ProQuest Ebook Central, p. 134. Retrieved at: http://ebookcentral.proquest.com/lib/gvsu/detail.action?docID=563858

Josephson, Jason Ananda, *The Invention of Religion in Japan*, The University of Chicago Press, Chicago and London, 2012. Print.

Khadra, Christelle, et al., "Projector-Based Virtual Reality Dome Environment for Procedural Pain and Anxiety in Young Children with Burn Injuries: A Pilot Study," *Journal of Pain Research* (2018), p. 11.

Klein, Julie Thompson, *Crossing Boundaries: Knowledge, Disciplinarities and Interdisciplinarities*, University Press of Virginia, Charlottesville and London, 1996. Print.

———, "Chapter Two: A Taxonomy of Interdisciplinarity," *The Oxford Handbook of Interdisciplinarity*, Robert Frodeman, editor, Oxford University Press, New York, 2010. Print.

Klein, Julie Thompson and Newell, William, "Advancing Interdisciplinary Studies," *Handbook of the Undergraduate Curriculum*, J. G. Gaff and J. Ratcliff, editors, Jossey-Bass, San Francisco, 1997, pp. 393–415. Print.

Knott, Kim, "Spatial Theory and Method for the Study of Religion," *Temenos*, Vol. 41, No. 2 (2005), pp. 153–184.

Kolowich, Steve, "The Water Next Time: Professor Who Helped Expose Crisis in Flint Says Public Science Is Broken," *Chronicle of Higher Education* (February 2, 2016). Retrieved at: http://chronicle.com/article/The-Water-Next-Time-Professor/235136

Komatsu, Koji, "Not Seeing is Believing: The Role of Invisibility in Human Lives," *Integrative Psychological Behaviour*, Vol. 51 (2017), pp. 14–28.

Larsen, Allan W., "The Phenomenology of Mircea Eliade," *Changing Religious Worlds: The Meaning and End of Mircea Eliade*, Bryan S. Rennie, editor, SUNY Press, Albany, 2001. Print.

Lattuca, Lisa R., *Creating Interdisciplinarity*, Vanderbilt University Press, Nashville, 2001. Print.

Markus, R. A., *Saeculum: History and Society in the Theology of St Augustine*, Cambridge University Press, Cambridge, UK, 1970. Print.

Martin, Luther H. and Wiebe, Donald, "Religious Studies as a Scientific Discipline: The Persistence of a Delusion," *Journal of the American Academy of Religion*, Vol. 82, No. 4 (December 2014).

Matthews, Eric, *The Philosophy of Merleau-Ponty*, Routledge, Abingdon, UK, 2002, ProQuest Ebook Central, p. 8. Retrieved at: http://ebookcentral.proquest.com/lib/gvsu/detail.action?docID=1900055

McCutcheon, Russell T., *Manufacturing Religion: The Discourse on Sui Generis Religion and the Politics of Nostalgia*, Oxford University Press, Oxford and New York, 1997. Print.

McGrath, Alister, *Christianity's Dangerous Idea*, HarperCollins, New York, 2007. Print.

104 *Bibliography*

McMullins, Neil, "The Encyclopedia of Religion: A Critique from the Perspective of the History of the Japanese Religious Traditions," *Method & Theory in the Study of Religion*, Vol. 1, No. 1 (Spring 1989), pp. 80–96.

The Medieval World 300–1300. Norman E. Cantor, editor, MacMillan Publishing Company, Inc., New York, 1968. Print.

Miller, Raymond C., "Varieties of Interdisciplinary Approaches in the Social Sciences: A 1981 Overview," *Issues in Integrative Studies*, No. 1 (1982).

Moran, Joe, *Interdisciplinarity*, Routledge, London, 2002. Print.

Morgan, David, *The Sacred Gaze: Religious Visual Culture in Theory and Practice*, University of California Press, Berkeley, 2005. Print.

———, *The Embodied Eye: Religious Visual Culture and the Social Life of Feeling*, University of California Press, Berkeley, 2012. Print.

———, "Material Analysis and the Study of Religion," *Materiality and the Study of Religion: The Stuff of the Sacred*, Tim Hutchings and Joanne McKenzie, editors, Routledge, London and New York, 2017. Print.

Morris, David, *The Sense of Space*, SUNY Press, Albany, 2004. Print.

———, *Merleau-Ponty's Developmental Ontology*, Northwestern University Press, Evanston, 2018. Print.

Nelson, Rebekah J., "Is Virtual Reality Exposure Therapy Effective for Service Members and Veterans Experiencing Combat-Related PTSD?," *Traumatology*, Vol. 19, No. 3 (2012), pp. 171–178.

Orsi, Robert A., *Between Heaven and Earth: The Religious Worlds People Make and the Scholars Who Study Them*, Princeton University Press, Princeton and Oxford, 2005. Print.

———, "Every Question Is Open: Looking for Paths Beyond the Clearing," *Critical Research on Religion*, Vol. 4, No. 3 (2016), pp. 260–266.

Pallasmaa, Juhani, *The Eyes of the Skin: Architecture and the Senses*, John Wiley and Sons, Hoboken, NJ, 2012. Print.

Parsons, Sarah and Mitchell, Peter "The Potential of Virtual Reality in Social Skills Training for People with Autistic Spectrum Disorders," *Journal of Intellectual Disability Research*, Vol. 46, Part 5, pp. 430–433, June 2002.

Pattison, Stephen, *Seeing Things: Deepening Relations with Visual Artefacts*, SCM Press, London, 2007. Print.

Pedersen, Olaf, *The First Universities: Studium Generale and the Origins of University Education in Europe*, Cambridge University Press, Cambridge, 1997. Print.

Preamble, "Association for Interdisciplinary Studies," Retrieved at: https://oakland.edu/ais/about/mission/

Presti, David E., *Mind Beyond Brain*, Columbia University Press, New York, 2018. Print.

Preston, Marilyn, "Autoethnography and Maternal Pedagogy: Storytelling Noncustodial Motherhood and Pedagogical Praxis," *Journal of Mother Studies*, No. 3 (September 2018).

Proudfoot, Wayne, "William James on an Unseen Order," *The Harvard Theological Review*, Vol. 93, No. 1 (January 2000).

Reat, N. Ross, "Insiders and Outsiders in the Study of Religious Traditions," *Journal of the American Academy of Religion*, Vol. 51, No. 3 (September 1, 1983), pp. 459–476, https://doi.org/10.1093/jaarel/LI.3.459

Bibliography 105

Repko, Allen F., *Interdisciplinary Research: Process and Theory*, Sage Publications, Inc., Los Angeles, 2012. Print.

Ricoeur, Paul, *Memory, History, Forgetting*, Kathleen Blamey and David Pellauer, trans., University of Chicago Press, Chicago, 2000. Print.

———, *The Course of Recognition*, David Pellauer, trans., Harvard University Press, Cambridge, MA, 2005. Print.

Rohlf, Michael, "Kant," *The Stanford Encyclopedia*, 2016. Retrieved at: https://plato.stanford.edu/entries/kant/

Rothbaum, Barbara O. and Hodges, Larry F., Ready, David, Graap, Ken, and Alarcon, Renato D., "Virtual Reality Exposure Therapy for Vietnam Veterans with Posttraumatic Stress Disorder," *Clinical Psychiatry*, (2001). Retrieved at: www.psychiatrist.com/JCP/article/Pages/2001/v62n08/v62n0808.aspx

Rovelli, Carlo, *The Order of Time*, Riverhead Books, New York, 2018. Print.

Smith, Jonathan Z., *Imagining Religion: From Babylon to Jonestown*, The University of Chicago Press, Chicago and London, 1982. Print.

———, "Religion, Religions, Religious," *Critical Terms for Religious Studies*, Mark C. Taylor, editor, The University of Chicago Press, Chicago, 1998. Print.

"Statutes of Gregory IX for the University of Paris in 1231," D.C. Munro, Translations and Reprints (Philadelphia: University of Pennsylvania Press), Vol II, No. 3, as quoted in *The Medieval World: 300–1300*, Norman F. Cantor, ed., Macmillan Publishing Company, Inc., 1968. Print.

"Statutes of Robert De Courcon for Paris in 1215," D.C. Munro, Translations and Reprints (Philadelphia: University of Pennsylvania Press), Vol II, No. 3, as quoted in *The Medieval World: 300–1300*, Norman F. Cantor, ed., Macmillan Publishing Company, Inc., 1968. Print.

Sullivan, H. P., "The History of Religions: Some Problems and Prospects," *The Study of Religion in Colleges and Universities*, Paul Ramsey and John F. Wilson, editors, Princeton University Press, Princeton, NJ, 1970. Print.

Tally, Robert T., Jr., *Spatiality*, Routledge Press, London and New York, 2013. Print.

Thorndike, Lynn, *University Records and Life in the Middle Ages*, Columbia University Press, New York, 1944. Print.

Toulmin, Stephen, *Return to Reason*, Harvard University Press, Cambridge, MA, 2001. Print.

Tracy, David, *Plurality and Ambiguity: Hermeneutics, Religion, and Hope*, Harper and Row, San Francisco, 1994. Print.

———, *The Analogical Imagination*, The Crossroads Publishing Company, New York, 1998, Print.

———, "The Ultimate Invisible: The Infinite," *Social Research*, Vol. 83, No. 4 (Winter 2016), pp. 879–880.

Walker, Caren and Gopnick, Alison, "Causality and Imagination." Retrieved at: http://alisongopnik.com/Papers_Alison/Causality%20and%20Imagination.pdf

Welch, James, IV, "The Emergence of Interdisciplinarity," *Issues in Integrative Studies*, Vol. 29 (2011), pp. 1–39.

Whitehead, Alfred North, *The Concept of Nature*, Project Gutenberg Ebook, 1919. Retrieved at: https://archives.library.illinois.edu/erec/University%20Archives/1515022/OriginalFiles/LITERATURE/WHITEHEAD/Concept%20of%20Nature%20Whitehead.pdf

106 *Bibliography*

————, *Religion in the Making*, The Macmillan Company, New York, 1926. Print.

————, *The Function of Reason*, Princeton University Press, Princeton, NJ, 1929. Print.

————, *Modes of Thought*, The MacMillan Company, New York, 1938. Print.

Wittman, Marc, *Felt Time: The Science of How We Experience Time*, The MIT Press, Cambridge, 2017. Print.

Zimbardo, Philip G. and Boyd, John N., "Putting Time in Perspective: A Valid, Reliable Individual-Differences Metric," *Journal of Personality and Social Psychology*, Vol. 77, No. 6 (1999), The American Psychological Association, Inc..

Index

Abelard, Peter 30
allegiances 29–30, 36, 42, 49, 57–58
anthropology 9
anxiety, exposure therapy 72–73
apparitions 76
architecture 75, 88–89
Association for Interdisciplinary
  Studies, definition of
  interdisciplinarity 26
Augustine 32, 33, 43, 51, 96; *On
  Christian Teaching* 32; *saeculum*
  51–52; "two books" 33–34
autoethnography 12, 13–14, 27, 37, 95

beliefs 24, 29, 34, 42, 52, 67;
  scientism 56
Blum, Jason 93
Book of Nature 52–53, 97
Book of Scripture 52–53, 97
boundaries 9, 10, 37, 47; between the
  sacred and profane 55–56
Boyd, John N. 71
Browning, Don 21
Bush, Vanevar 35

cathedral university 29–30, 33
chancellor 30
characteristics of interdisciplinarity 4
*Charrtularium universitatis
  Parieiensis* 32
Chicago School 56
Christendom 34; Augustine 43;
  monasteries 30
Christianity 28, 31, 34, 35, 42, 95,
  96, 97; Book of Scripture 52–53,

97; Protestant Reformation 33, 52,
  92; and religion 50–51; two-world
  hypothesis 55
Church, the 30
City of God 51, 52
City of Man 51, 52
"class language" 24
Clebsch, William 16
collaboration 38; allegiances 49;
  interdisciplinary 38–39
colonialism 92, 96; European 42
computers 19
*Condemnation of Errors at Paris in
  1241* 30
consciousness 28, 56; *see also* self-
  consciousness
constructivism 60, 80
counterfactual 5
critical philosophy 54
cultural studies 38

deconstructionism 80
delusions 76–77
disciplines 9, 10, 29, 30, 32, 36, 38–39,
  43; and multidisciplinarity 61;
  multidisciplinarity 39–40; synthesis
  40–41
Doniger, Wendy 86
Durkheim, Emile 43, 55, 59

education 34, 52, 97
Eliade, Mircea 10, 11, 14, 21, 42, 43,
  54, 56, 57, 58, 62, 67, 80; *The Sacred
  and the Profane: The Nature of
  Religion* 43, 57; *see also* hierophany

108 *Index*

embodiment 20
empirical science 28–29
encyclopedie 32
Enlightenment, the 2, 16, 18, 28–29, 32, 34, 35, 53, 54, 92, 97
epistemological project, university as 1, 3, 6, 15, 16–18, 27–37, 41, 48–50, 52, 57–60, 92–93, 96–97, 100
epistemology 2, 93; and reason 53–54; unitary function of 28–29
ethnography 13–14
European universities 29, 30
experience 55–56, 94; autoethnography 27; religious 28; residing in time in an unseen order 71–75; in the sacred-profane domain 65–66
"experience error" 70
exposure therapy 72, 74, 80; virtual reality environments (VREs) 65, 75
extra-disciplinary epistemological assemblages 61

faith 24, 92
formulation 28, 34

Gabriel, Markus 60
Gilkey, Langdon 21
God 28
Grand Valley State University (GVSU) 23, 29
guilds 30
Gustafson, James 16

Habermas, Jurgen 93, 100
hallucinations 77
Hegel, G. W. F. 34
Heidegger, Martin 69
hermeneutics 24
hierophany 3, 20, 56, 66, 85, 87, 88, 90–91
History of Religions 16, 42, 43, 54, 56, 58
human activity 58; *see also* insider activity; profane, the; sacred, the; secular, the
human nature 67
Hume, David 92
hypotheses 28

identity 13, 14, 49, 65; sense of presence 71–72
illusions 76–77

immersion 66, 67, 71–72, 75, 77, 78; virtual reality environments (VREs) 63
inquiry 10, 28, 30, 33, 36, 40, 41, 44, 49; of GVSU's religious studies program 23–24
insider activity 69; immersion 72; recognition 77–78, 79; residing inside a VRE 80–81; and the sacred-profane domain 65–66; and the unseen order 66
insider/outsider domains 24, 27, 38, 40, 85, 86; and the sacred-profane domain 65–66
integration, disciplinary 40–41
intellectual history of the university 2, 3, 10–11, 17, 18, 25, 29, 30, 35; Augustine 32; cathedral university 33
intention 70
interdisciplinarity 3, 4, 9, 12–13, 17, 19, 21, 23, 25, 26, 27, 29, 37, 38, 42, 43–44, 48–49, 50, 54, 59, 61, 65–66, 67, 69, 74, 77, 83, 88, 93, 95, 96, 98, 99; autoethnography 12; boundaries 9, 10; and location 4–12; situatedness 14; synthesis 40–41; and the unseen order 20
interdisciplinary collaboration 38–39
interpretation 7, 83; similarity-in-difference 69
Invective Against the New Learning, An 30
invisibility 68–69, 70, 71
Islam 95

James, William 12, 91, 93, 99; *The Varieties of Religious Experience* 20, 67, 68; *see also* unseen order, the

Kant, Immanuel 34, 53, 54; *Critique of Practical Reason* 54; *Critique of Pure Reason* 54; *Critique of the Power of Judgment* 54
Klein, Julie Thompson 26
knowledge 1, 4, 8, 14, 30, 32, 34, 36, 60, 87, 93; gathering 91–92; and location 4–12; and reason 53–54; and recognition 65–66, 76, 90; recognition 77, 77–78, 79; scientific

33; self- 83; silos 15, 26, 93, 100; and study 10; and thinking 89
knowledge production 12–13, 15, 17–18, 25, 26, 28, 35, 38, 50, 54, 88, 91, 95, 96; synthesis 40–41

language 15; "class" 24; and hierophany 87; and the modern study of religion 42; and time 73–74
liberal arts education 8
libraries 27, 32, 97
life and death domains 47–48, 61–62, 65
liminal 15
Lived Religion 3
location 12–13, 21, 23, 24, 26, 28, 30, 31, 37, 39, 40, 42, 44, 48–49, 60, 62, 71, 83, 86, 87, 91; importance and complexity of 4–12; and interpretation 7; and invisibility 70; and recognition 79; self-consciousness of 6–7, 10, 12, 17, 95; situatedness 13, 14–15; two-world hypothesis 51

macrocosmos 32
Marty, Martin 21
Marx, Karl 35, 60
Material Religion 3, 94
McCutcheon, Russell 54, 57, 80
meaning 8
medieval universities 29–30, 32, 50, 92
memory 86–87
Merleau-Ponty, Maurice 20, 69
metaphysics 60, 98
methodology 1, 7, 25, 30, 36, 37, 48, 87, 91, 93, 95, 98; in religious studies 3
microcosmos 32
modern university 43–44, 61–62
monasteries 30, 52
Moran, Joe 26; *Interdisciplinarity* 41, 93
Morgan, David 76, 89, 94
multidisciplinarity 25, 39–40, 61; synthesis 40–41
mysterium tremendum 55

natural religion 10–11, 35, 42, 49, 92
natural sciences 55–56
nature 52–53
Neusner, Jacob 16
New Realism 19

objectivity 13, 68–69, 76, 99
ocularcentrism 68–69
organizing function of universities 28, 31–33, 34, 35, 37, 38, 49
Orsi, Robert 83–84, 92, 99, 100
Otto, Rudolf 55
overlapping domain of the sacred-profane 19, 62–63, 68–69, 71, 80–81, 85, 88, 90–91; *see also* profane, the; sacred, the; sacred-profane domain

Pallasmaa, Juhani 75
personal history 12
phenomena 84–85, 91, 99; apparitions 76; religious 55–56
phenomenology 55–56, 87
philosophy 2, 3, 8, 10–11, 24, 28, 29, 34, 35, 36, 52, 54, 92, 96, 97; phenomenology 55–56; pietistic reductionism 56–57; positivism 56
pietistic reductionism 56–57
place 87, 88; *see also* space
political science 38, 49
positionality 5, 12, 12–13, 15, 17–18, 21, 26, 49, 50, 54, 61, 85; scholarly 83; situatedness 13, 14–15
positivism 36, 56
postmodernism 43
post-traumatic stress disorder (PTSD) 72, 73, 80; exposure therapy 75
presentism 73
Presti, David, *Mind Beyond Brain* 70
profane, the 3, 17, 19, 20, 29, 43, 48, 49, 54, 55, 57, 58, 59, 71, 80, 85; hierophany 20; *saecularizatio* 50–51; two-world hypothesis 55; *see also* sacred-profane domain
Protestant Reformation 33, 92
public policy 38

Ramsey, Paul 16
"reality" 71
reason 53
recognition 65–66, 76, 77, 77–78, 79, 85, 87, 90
reductionism 19, 40–41, 55–56, 58; pietistic 56–57
reflection 29, 38, 79, 89
Reformation, the 18, 33, 52, 92
"Religion and Popular Culture" course 67–69

110 *Index*

religion 2, 3, 9, 12–13, 16, 17, 22n20, 23, 24, 26, 27, 28, 29, 33, 35, 37, 38, 40, 43, 49, 54, 96, 99; Book of Scripture 52–53; as Christian theology 35–36; and education 52; modern study of 42; monasteries 29–30; "natural" 92; pietistic reductionism 56–57; and space 51–52; and time 50; two-world hypothesis 51, 55; universalizing the sacred 61–62; and the unseen order 20

"Religion and Love" course 84

Religion and the Body 3

religious studies 1, 2, 12–13, 17, 19, 21, 25, 37, 38, 42, 44, 69, 74, 80, 81, 95, 96, 99–100; GVSU program 23, 29; interdisciplinarity 27; and life and death domains 47–48; location 4–12; methodology 3; positionality 17–18; rise of 41–44; and the unseen order 20

research: autoethnography 27; interdisciplinarity 38

residence 66, 69, 88; immersive 66–67; in space in the unseen order 75–79; in time in the unseen order 71–75; in the unseen order 70

retooling 67

Ricouer, Paul 65, 66, 76, 77

ring giving and receiving 85–86, 87, 89, 90, 94

rise of religious studies 41–44

sacred, the 3, 9, 14–15, 17, 19, 20, 29, 43, 48, 49, 54, 55, 57, 58, 59, 71, 80, 85; City of God 51; hierophany 20, 56, 88; and recognition 63–64; two-world hypothesis 55; universalizing 60, 61, 62; *see also* sacred-profane domain

sacred-profane domain 62–63, 65–66, 88; retooling 67

saecularizatio 50–51

saeculum 51–52

scholasticism 8, 9–10, 10, 12, 27, 38, 40, 81, 91, 96; and identity 14; liminal 15; positionality 83; self-consciousness 24, 48–49, 85

schools 30

science 2, 10–11, 17, 28, 29, 33, 35, 36, 37, 49, 52, 92, 96, 97; empirical 28–29

Science: The Endless Frontier 35

scientism 56, 57, 93, 100

secular, the 49, 58; City of Man 51; *saecularizatio* 50–51; *saeculum* 51–52; *see also* profane, the

secularis 50

Self, the 87

self-consciousness 6–7, 24, 26, 37, 48–49, 83, 95; of location 10, 12, 17; scholarly 85; "third way" 83–84

self-knowledge 13, 83

semiotics 8

sense of presence 71–72, 75; and exposure therapy 72–73

similarity-in-difference 69

simultaneity 19, 66

situatedness 13, 21, 76, 89

Smith, Jonathan Z. 6, 11, 92

social constructionism 3, 19, 43, 54, 57, 58, 67

social groups 55

social sciences 24, 42, 49, 55–56, 97

space 87; immersion 75, 76, 77; in an unseen order, residing in 75–79; *see also* immersion

specialization 58, 97

Stendahl, Krister 16

study 10

subjectivity 13, 76, 99

Sullivan, H. P. 16–17

sympathetic inquiry 10

synthesis 40–41, 41

teachers 30

technology, virtual reality environments (VREs) 67, 68, 69

Technology Showcase 67–68, 70, 74

theology 2–3, 10–11, 23, 24, 30, 31, 33, 34, 35, 42, 52, 80, 91–92, 96; Augustine 43; Book of Scripture 52–53; of Eliade 57

theories 28

thinking 89

"third way" 83–84, 99

Thomas, George F. 16

time 70, 87, 88; and language 73–74; presentism 73; and religion 50;

Index 111

secularis 50; situatedness 89; in an unseen order, residing in 71–75
Time Perspectives 71
Tracy, David 6, 7, 21, 24, 25, 79
traumatic events, exposure therapy 72, 74–75, 80
truth 13
"two books" 33–34, 43
two-world hypothesis 43, 50, 51, 52–53, 55

universalizing the sacred 60, 61, 62
universals 30–31
universitas 27, 34, 50, 57, 92, 97
universities 1, 12–13, 16, 17, 19, 28, 30, 31, 33, 36, 40, 42, 48, 52, 54, 57, 59, 67, 81, 85, 93, 96, 98, 99; allegiances 29–30, 36, 49; chancellor 30; chief ordering structure 19; disciplines 43; epistemological development of 2, 88; epistemological function 28–29; European 29, 30; Grand Valley State University (GVSU) 23; importance and complexity of location 4–12; insider/outsider 27; intellectual history of 2, 3, 10–11, 18; interdisciplinarity 26, 41; interdisciplinary collaboration 39; medieval 29–30, 50, 92; modern 43–44, 61–62; organizing function of 31–33, 34, 35, 37, 38, 49; positionality 49, 50; and the Reformation 52–53; "Religion and Popular Culture" class 67–69; "Religion and Love" course 84; research 97; scholars 8–9; two-world hypothesis 51; Western 28, 96

unseen order, the 4, 20, 66, 67, 68, 88, 89; recognition 77–78; residing in 70; residing in space in 75–79; residing in time in 71–75

vicious intellectualism 99
virtual reality environments (VREs) 20, 67, 70, 78, 79–80; exposure therapy 65, 72, 73, 74; immersion 72, 75; "Religion and Popular Culture" class 67–69; sense of presence 71–72

Western universities 28, 29, 30, 96
Whitehead, Alfred North 27, 54, 92, 98
Wilson, John F. 16
Wittman, Marc, *Felt Time: The Science of How We Experience Time* 71

Zimbardo, Philip G. 71

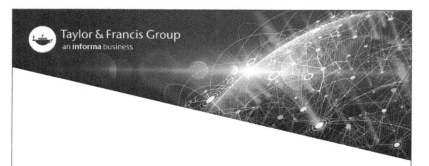